RECOLLECTIONS OF
Charley Russell

D0190542

RECOLLECTIONS OF
Charley Russell

BY FRANK BIRD LINDERMAN

Edited and with an introduction by H. G. Merriam

WITH DRAWINGS BY

CHARLEY RUSSELL

UNIVERSITY OF OKLAHOMA PRESS : *Norman and London*

LIBRARY OF CONGRESS CATALOG CARD NUMBER: 63–18074
ISBN: 0–8061–0582–8
ISBN: 0–8061–2112–2 (pbk.)

5   6   7   8   9   10   11   12   13   14   15   16   17   18   19   20

TO THE MEMORY OF THE MEN AND WOMEN

WHO MADE LIFE IN THE EARLY WEST PLUNGE AND REAR

AND TO THOSE WHO GENTLED IT.

—H.G.M.

INTRODUCTION

These recollections carry a fresh look at the cowboy artist, Charles M. Russell, recounted by a long-time companion and close friend, Frank Bird Linderman. Not one of the biographers of Russell has tapped this source, although Nancy Russell wished to include her husband's letters to Linderman in her collection published as Good Medicine.[1]

The meeting of the two men was several years after their outdoor experiences, when they were both married and at work as family men. Russell was settling into steady painting, his cowboy days behind him; Linderman was, in succession, an assayer, a businessman, a newspaper owner and editor, a legislator, and an insurance agent before he could settle down and become a writer about Plains Indians and early Western life.

How the men happened to meet I do not know. Linderman states that they met about the time of Charley's marriage, which was in 1896. The meeting was inevitable—if not at that time, then later—for they had so much in

[1] On March 21, 1928, Nancy Russell wrote to Linderman that she was collecting her husband's letters to be "put into a book" (*Good Medicine: A Biographical Note* [New York, 1929]). "You have, I think, the finest collection of letters anyone has which were written by Charley. . . . If you will let me have them . . . I will return the originals to you [after plates have been made]. As I say, I believe yours are the best." Linderman had had experience with letting materials go out of his hands, even with Nancy, and proposed having the letters photographed in Kalispell (March 27, 1928). Nancy responded on

common. Not even the stretches of Montana miles could have kept them unknown to one another.

Both men came west in the early 1880's as lads about sixteen years of age and entered into a primitive way of living, passionately eager for the experience. Linderman was a trapper and guide for hunters for about eight years, and Russell was a cowboy for nearly twice that number of years. Neither boy ran away from home, as has sometimes been asserted, for each had the consent of his father, Linderman's even riding a short way with him on the westbound train and Charley's sending him with a friend and supplying him with money.

Russell would not attend school—he played hookey successfully one time for several weeks—but, living in St. Louis, a city full of hardy men of the West, he soaked up their experiences and wild tales of the wide-open country, Indians, buffalo, grizzly bears, and herds of wild cattle. Linderman as a youth pored over maps to discover the spot in the United States "most remote from civilization."

April 3: "Your reluctance in letting your precious original letters out of your hand is understood by me and the responsibility I was putting on my own shoulders in having the nerve to ask for them must be understood by you. . . . But, if you feel that you cannot trust your treasures to leave your hands, I will be happy to get the photographs, which will mean that your particular letters will be in black and white. . . . It seems a shame not to have as many of Charley's letters as possible under one cover." Linderman had to go east on a lecture tour at that time, and no letters to him appeared in *Good Medicine*.

viii

Both as callow youths met up with older men, Russell with Jake Hoover, an old-time mountain man with whom he lived and learned for two years and to whose cabin and companionship he returned again and again as to home, and Linderman with a trapper, Alvin Lee, like Hoover a much older man but perhaps not so instructive a one.

On the range Russell lived the rugged and demanding life of the cowboy; in town he seemingly lived the usual rowdy life of the times, drinking,[2] going on sprees, and visiting the houses of the madams. Between seasons for open-air work, like other cowboys, he holed up on some ranch—no cowboy was then refused hospitality—or in a town until spring broke out of winter and herding began again. Linderman's experience as a trapper cast him among fewer men and less often into town life. Linderman married at twenty-four years of age in 1893, Russell at thirty-two in 1896.

Both men when young spent time with Plains Indians, Russell with the Bloods in Canada, a branch of the Blackfeet Indians, Linderman with the Flatheads first, then

---

[2] Harold McCracken (*The Charles M. Russell Book* [Garden City, N.Y., 1957]) states on page 205 that "by 1908 . . . he had given up drinking." He may have done so earlier.

with the Blackfeet, and later with the Cree and Chippewa tribes. Both greatly respected the old-time Indian, his way of life, his love of fun, his beliefs, and perhaps most of all his co-operation with nature, his adjustment to it.

If the two met in 1897 or thereabouts, Linderman would have been living in Butte, Montana, as an assayer for the Butte and Boston Smelter, and Russell would have been in Great Falls as a painter. Between the time of their meeting and 1905 they probably were together seldom, but between 1905 and 1917, when Linderman was living in Helena, meetings were no doubt more frequent, Russell probably being in and out of the capital city and Linderman on business at Great Falls. Their camping trips together probably took place then and certainly later. In 1917, Linderman built his house on Goose Bay on Flathead Lake, and to it Russell often came to visit the family —"almost every year," one member of it wrote—and to prepare for his camping trips with Frank.[3]

It would be difficult to state which of the two men was the better storyteller. Russell wrote in the Foreword to

[3] See the recollections by Verne Linderman in the Appendices to this volume.

his Rawhide Rawlins,[4] *"Where there's nothing to read men must talk, so when they were gathered at ranches or stage stations, they amused themselves with tales of their own or others' adventures." He might as truthfully have added, "tales of their invention." Like all good tales, theirs probably grew with the retelling. Both enjoyed the appreciation of listeners. Each when with each other or with other storytellers, like men everywhere, vied in telling the best story. Will Rogers and Irvin S. Cobb, both friends of Russell's, thought him "one of the most accomplished storytellers in America." They would have made the same comment had they heard Frank Linderman.*

Both men became professional artists, Russell in paint and clay and bronze and Linderman in words. Both used similar subject matter. The paintings, sketches, and sculptures of Russell ran into the thousands. Linderman wrote seven books about the Plains Indians, their tales, legends, and myths; a children's story of a chipmunk; five novels of early Western life, two of them published and three unpublished; a thin volume of verse; and several articles

[4] Great Falls, Mont., 1921.

xi

for periodicals. Both men wrote verse, although neither possessed the genuine poetic gift.

In sum, Charles Marion Russell and Frank Bird Linderman took to one another because of their natures and their experiences, their love of "unspoiled" country and "unspoiled" people, especially Indians, and because both had a passion for preserving Western life as it was twenty years and more before the turn of the century. No doubt Linderman joined Russell heartily in saying, "I'm glad I lived when I did—not twenty years later. I saw things when they were new." This was not quite true—but both thought it was—for by 1880 "unspoiled" life in the West was on the wane.

It is strange that biographers of Russell have not tapped the Linderman materials, strange that they have not realized, if they knew of it, what this close relationship may have meant to Russell. Ramon F. Adams and Homer E. Britzman,[5] without naming him, refer to the letter which Linderman wrote to Russell, the occasion for which resulted in a temporary falling out between them. Harold

[5] *Charles M. Russell, The Cowboy Artist* (Pasadena, Calif., 1948).

McCracken and Lola Shelton[6] *ignore Linderman, although the former lists him as among Russell's friends. Austin Russell*[7] *mentions Linderman and recounts the Missouri River trip which is told in detail in this volume.*

Frank Bird Linderman (1869–1938) hailed from Ohio and Chicago. As a young lad in Ohio he would tramp off from home to hunt squirrels with his sawed-off musket over his shoulder. It was doubtless the later Chicago days and the natural response of youth to romance which created in him a hankering to get away from "contaminating civilization." The hankering became determination, as with Russell, and at sixteen years of age, after persuading his parents to let him go west, he found himself alone in a leaking cabin in Flathead Indian country in western Montana. The rain came on and on; he had cut his foot to the bone by accidentally stepping on an ax blade; his grub was almost gone; his only possessions were a light overcoat, an ax, and an old percussion-lock Kentucky rifle. "I felt mighty blue," he understated in later years.

[6] Shelton, *Charles Marion Russell: Cowboy, Artist, Friend* (New York, 1962).
[7] *Charles M. Russell: Cowboy Artist* (New York, 1957).

However, he stuck it out; met his first Indian, a Flathead
"who had taken more scalps than any other members of
his tribe" and who instinctively knew he was "a rank pil-
grim . . . a babe in the woods"; became a trapper, first
with a white man and later successively with two Indians,
and a guide for hunters.[8]

   The eight years he spent in this rugged work gave him
experiences which he always treasured. He loved the free-
dom of the life, the outdoorness of it, the birds and animals,
the silence, the long days and evenings of summers, the
crisp, invigorating air of springs and autumns, the streams
and the mountains and the long tramps beside and over
them. He loved nature untouched by man; he hated ex-
ploitation of it.

   When he met Minnie Jane Johns, love for her and love
of the untrammeled outdoor life pulled him two ways.
After a year of itching feet and yearning spirit he married
her, and with marriage came return to civilization, that
of Montana in the 1890's. He engaged in several occu-
pations during the next ten or twelve years, learning, in

[8] See H. G. Merriam, "Sign-Talker with a Straight Tongue," *Montana, The Magazine of Western History*, Vol. XII, No. 3 (Summer, 1962), 2–20.

the valued early Western way, from experience. Before marriage he had tended store in old Demersville, had gone to the Curley mine near Victor, Montana, to be its watchman and found himself becoming its bookkeeper and assayer. (He had sent off for books and taught himself.) Soon after marriage he became, as has been noted, an assayer in Butte. In 1898 he moved his family to Sheridan, Montana, living just outside of it in Brandon, and there he owned and ran a small furniture store, owned and edited the town's paper, Chinook, *and prospected, unsuccessfully, at odd times. In 1903 and again in 1905 he was elected a representative in the Montana legislature. From 1905 to 1917 he lived in Helena, Montana, as an insurance salesman. The acquaintances made during the legislative sessions were valuable to him as an insurance man. Although by nature not at all a politician, being outspoken and little given to circumspection, he found himself an assistant secretary of state and later the Republican candidate, in 1916 and again in 1918, for election to the U.S. House of Representatives and, after he had left Helena,*

for the U.S. Senate.[9] *In 1917, he had accumulated sufficient money to build a commodious, beautiful log house
on Goose Bay on the shore of large Flathead Lake. This
was precarious, for by this time there were three daughters
to be educated. But he was determined to write, he had
enough money to see the family through several years,
and he hoped to make a living from the books he would
produce.*

*In Helena his interest in Indians widened. Previously
his experience had been chiefly with the Flatheads of western Montana and with the Blackfeet across the Divide;
now his association was mainly with the penniless, wandering tribes of Crees and Chippewas. Together with other
citizens, among them Charley Russell, he interested himself in getting a reservation for them, spending many
weeks one year at his own expense in Washington, D.C.,
in their behalf. There he was told that nothing would be
done, for "the Indian has no vote," but finally the tribes
were settled upon a new reservation, the Rocky Boy in*

[9] Linderman was defeated in 1916 for Representative by Jeannette Rankin,
the first woman to be elected to the U.S. Congress and the only Representative
to vote against U.S. entry into World War I. In 1918 he was defeated by John
M. Evans. In a letter to Frank, Charley wrote: ". . . I am mighty sorry you
lost out but loosings ar some times winings for som political jobs has tor
down mor men than it built up[.] Im speaking of men I know that held
offices[.] I had no chance to vote for you but I shure ribbed[.] I voted for Dock
[O. M. Lanstrum, candidate for the Senate] but it seems like my ribben an

northern Montana.[10] *The Indians never lost their gratitude for the aid Linderman had given them and turned
to him later and often in difficulties that came to them.*
  *During this association the Crees and Chippewas filled
his mind with tales, customs, beliefs, legends, myths of
their tribes. Opie Read, whose novel* The Jucklins *was
said to have sold over one million copies, visited Helena
in 1911 and Linderman put on a dinner for him at the
Montana Club, doubtless pouring out Indian lore. When
again he met Read, in Forsyth, Montana, in 1914, the
author's farewell remark was, "Go at it . . . print the Indian lore." Before leaving Helena for Goose Bay in 1917
he had written* Indian Why Stories, *legends and tales of
the Blackfeet, Cree, and Chippewa tribes, and Charles
Scribner's Sons had published it in 1915. Linderman wrote
to Russell asking him to illustrate the book and he had
agreed, saying: "I received your letter and am glad you
got across with your storyes[.] I will be glad to do the
cover designs and Marginals and you can pay me out of*

voating was bad medison[.] I must have passed the pipe across the door or
forgot to smoke with the sun." Linderman's successful opponent for the U.S.
Senate in 1917 was Thomas J. Walsh.

  [10] The Linderman heirs have given to The Museum of the Plains Indian
in Browning, Montana, the Frank B. Linderman Collection of Indian Correspondence consisting of "more than 500 letters, telegrams, memoranda, legislative bills, field notes and other papers." The majority of these materials "relate
to the destitution of landless Indians of Montana, the long continued efforts

your first royalty and I'l promise you not to tap the snap[.]
Id kind a like to turn the leaves of that book my self[.]
Il go to work right away[.] *with bes wishes to all your
friend."* On June 16, 1915, *Linderman wrote Russell: ". . .
you will see by the terms that they are going to offer me
that there is no money in the book for me, but it will give
me a big boost . . . I have landed nicely and that is what
I want."*[11] *Like all beginning writers he mistook a first
acceptance for continued success, and save for a reprint of
this book into a school edition,* Indian Lodge-Fire Stories
*(1918), it was five years before another publication came
to him. In the next fifteen years four similar books followed one another:* Indian Old-Man Stories *(1920), illustrated by Russell;* How It Came About Stories *(1921), the
only book in which any of the tales are his own invention,*[12] Kootenai Why Stories *(1926), illustrated by C. L.
Bull; and* Old-Man Coyote Stories *(1931), illustrated by
H. M. Stoops. The sale of the books was slow and not
large. Linderman more than once said to me, "The critics
all praise my books, but the public won't buy them."* Over

---

to secure some land for them and their eventual settlement upon the Rocky
Boy Reservation." Notice released by the Museum on Feb. 15, 1963.

[11] Letters under the care of Norma Linderman Waller, Kalispell, Montana.

the years he became embittered. Telling him that people were then not really interested in Indians was of no avail.

In 1931 the John Day Company, whose president Richard Walsh he had interested during a visit of several months in New York City, published American: The Life Story of a Great Indian, Plenty-Coups, Chief of the Crows, *illustrated by H. M. Stoops, who became an ardent admirer of Linderman and his writing. Linderman had interviewed Plenty-Coups on the Crow Reservation through an interpreter, checking the translation by his own knowledge of the sign language which the old full-blood used as he talked. He wished, as far as possible, to recapture Plains Indian life before it was irreparably influenced by white contacts. He did not trust half-bloods or young Indians, convinced that they knew too little about old days and ways. Fortunately, Linderman was a creative listener.*

American *is a genuinely valuable book for anyone wishing to learn of Plains Indian life. The New York* Times *reviewer noted that "nothing altogether comparable . . . has heretofore been added to our literature concerning*

---

[12] Mrs. Waller said to me: "I remember so well Daddy's coming from his desk into the living room and triumphantly reading a new, good story to us."

the American Indian." It was followed by Red Mother
*(1933), written to illuminate the Indian woman's life.
Linderman interviewed Pretty Shield, the red mother, as
he had Plenty-Coups, checking the sign language carefully. Plenty-Coups issued the following statement, which
was published in the book about him: "I am glad I have
told you these things, Sign-Talker. You have felt my heart
and I have felt yours. I know you will tell only what I
have said, that your writing will be straight like your
tongue, and I sign your paper with my thumb so that your
people and mine will know I told you the things you have
written down." Pretty Shield commented for the book
about her: "I told Sign-Talker the things that are in this
book, and have signed them with my thumb."*[13]

*Linderman knew Plains Indians as friends whom he ad-
mired. He also, being curious about their inner life as well
as the outer, before white contamination, treasured their
legends and beliefs and their relationship to all that is in
heaven and on earth.*

Although Linderman's principal interest was in Indians,

[13] Professor Robert H. Lowie, in his review of the book in *The American
Anthropologist* (Vol. XXXVI, No. 1 [Jan.-Mar., 1934], 124–26), questioned the
accuracy of some remarks on the Sun Dance made to Linderman by Pretty
Shield. Linderman took great pains and expense to make correction when,
after a trip to the Crow Reservation, he discovered that the criticism had been
justified.

his interest in preserving in fiction the life of the old West led to the writing of five novels, two of which were published, Lige Mounts: Free Trapper *(1922; reprinted in 1932 with the title* Morning Light, *by the John Day Company) and* Beyond Law *(1933). The critic Frederic F. Van de Water placed these novels "in the first rank of novels of the West."*[14] *Interest in animals, which was always keen with him, led to the writing of* Stumpy *(1933), a biography of a chipmunk which acted out its life before Linderman's study window.*

Frank Bird Linderman was one of Montana's most accomplished writers.[15] *He possessed a fine conscience in his effort to interpret the red man, an almost fanatically painstaking regard for accuracy, a sense of form, and an ear for language. His writing has lasting value and should be more widely known than it is.*

Charley Russell as an artist was equally scrupulous about detailed accuracy. The beadwork, for instance, on a moccasin or a headband had to be authentic to its tribe, as did

[14] *Frontier and Midland,* Vol. XIX, No. 3 (Spring, 1939), 148–52.

[15] A Russell letter to Linderman is of interest. It is dated January 31, 1918: ". . . I suppose by this time your getting along with your book in fine shape[.] that country of yours [Flathead Lake] is shure the place to bring storys to a man[.] every where you look is another page in old lady natures story book to those how [who] can read her writing and you know her hand write. and have listened when she read out loude."

details of saddles and designs on robes, and especially the bones and muscles of animals and men. Russell learned anatomy not from books or in the laboratory but, from his earliest days in St. Louis to his last in Great Falls, from steady observation and countless drawings and moldings of animals and men. Frank once asked him if he ever worked from models; the question, asked in the studio, almost answered itself as he watched Charley at work— he would have worn out a model. Charley said that sometimes he would mold a model in clay and paint from it.

Charles Marion Russell (1864–1926) was born in St. Louis.[16] *Coming to Montana in 1880, he lived the free life of the cowboy of that time. He played the game as it was; to him it was play, and he enjoyed every minute of it. In* Trails Plowed Under, *and in the Preface to* More Rawhides *he wrote: "I have always been a good mixer—I had friends when I had nothing else. Life has never been too serious with me. I have lived to play and I'm playing yet [1925, the year before his death]. I believe in luck and I've had a lot of it."*

[16] Nancy Russell in a letter to Linderman dated June 17, 1912, wrote: "Chas' birthday was the 19th day of March, 1865. He was born on Olive Street, Saint Louis. He came to Helena by stage the first part of March, 1880. He does not remember the exact day." In another letter dated June 12, without the year, she had written: "Chas. was born at St. Louis in 1865." In her biographical note in *Good Medicine* she gave the date as 1864. *Who's Who in*

Life with the Bloods in 1888 instilled in him admiration for their simple living, their love of fun, their honesty among themselves, their reverence for nature and beliefs in spiritual forces. To them some animals were smarter than men, faster in movement, clearer and keener in vision, and they gave the animals credit for those qualities. Pretty much dispossessed by the white man, the Bloods aroused Russell's sympathy and his indignation against the white man. He did not, however, see as deeply into the Indians' inner life as Linderman did; he knew their outward life. His biographers state that he was tempted to throw in his lot with them and spend his life as an Indian. His wife Nancy, in her biographical note in Good Medicine, *stated: "The Red Men of the Northwest [really the Blackfeet and the Crees and Chippewas] love and think of Charlie as a kind of medicine man because he drew them and their life so well."*

Russell's life toned down when he married Nancy in 1896. She measured his drinks for him when he went downtown by holding up fingers for him to indicate the

America records the date as 1865. Library of Congress catalog cards carry the date as 1864.

number he might take, and she kept his former companions away from him as much as possible. Con Price, a long-time friend and ranch partner, in Trails I Rode, *has another friend of Charley's, John Mathison, a freighter, say "one cold winter day" that he had not seen Charley since his marriage because the "damn woman (Nancy) was always in the way." That no doubt represented the feeling of most of Russell's former pals.*

His wife made him see something of the value of his paintings, but she could not make him into a salesman of them. She herself became the salesman, demanding and getting prices that made Charley gasp. In 1903 she took him on his first trip to New York City to sell his paintings. There he met artists and other prominent men, like Bill Hart, but he could not be comfortable in spirit in "the big tipi." Soon the trips became almost annual. The prices of his pictures went up and up.

Charley preferred to be in his "shack," his "medicine tipi," painting and talking to friends. He worked diligently under the urging of "Mame," his wife. An inex-

haustible number of scenes out of his first decade and a half in Montana supplied him with subjects for his brush and his fingers. His paintings and sculptures alike usually showed movement—the bronco bucking, the freighter moving his ox team and wagon over arid land and mountain passes, white men and Indian scouts on the hunt, tricks played by cowboys, a grizzly bear on a rampage— on and on and on.

Over the years one sees improvement in his painting, principally in an obviously more serious attitude toward his art, but from the beginning his work was authentic and striking. He had become Western through and through, in appearance, in actions, in ideas, in attitudes, in speech. Nancy Russell said that it took her a long time to understand her husband's lingo. Every action of his, every word he uttered was, like his every picture and sculpture, unmistakably early Western. His animals were those habiting east of the Continental Divide. Whether on paper or canvas or in beeswax, clay, or bronze they were active, alive. This partially accounts for his popularity as an artist.

K. Ross Toole has aptly expressed another reason, namely, a sort of nostalgia or perhaps a feeling of the capture of something gone: "The entire product of Charles M. Russell is an eternal commentary on the end of a great and important American experience."[17]

Russell's paintings, at least in the West, have received more acclaim than his sculptures, but in the long run his sculptures more than his paintings will be valued by artists.

Frank Linderman had told me of his recollections of Charley Russell several times before he allowed me to publish extracts from them, selected by him, in Frontier and Midland *(a regional magazine which I was editing and publishing from 1927 to 1939) but not until recently had I seen the whole manuscript. Some years ago J. Frank Dobie had seen the manuscript when visiting in Kalispell, Montana, where the Linderman papers are in the care of Norma Linderman Waller.*

The eldest daughter, Miss Wilda Linderman, did not think that the recollections should be published because

---

[17] Quoted by Michael Kennedy in the Introduction to Shelton, *op. cit.*

her father had written them during a period of discouragement and illness and they were not expressed in the finished language which he normally achieved. And her sisters, Miss Verne Linderman and Mrs. Roy Waller, agreed that publication of the manuscript as it existed would not redound to the reputation of their father.

When my article entitled "Sign-Talker with a Straight Tongue" appeared in Montana, The Magazine of Western History, in the summer of 1962, J. Frank Dobie wrote me that in his judgment the recollections should be published. I had long hoped that they might be, for I had known Frank Linderman for the last eighteen years of his life and had read some of his writings in manuscript and all of his published works, had visited many times in the Goose Bay home, and had heard Frank talk much about Russell. I wrote the three sisters, whom I had known both in the family and as college students, suggesting that I be allowed to rework the manuscript, since I believed I had insight into the nature of Linderman's use of English. I hastily rewrote a page of the manuscript, which had been *sent to me for reading, and enclosed it in my letter as a suggestion of what might be done. The sisters somewhat reluctantly allowed me to edit the entire manuscript. They readily saw, since Charley Russell was becoming, as a recent writer in* Holiday *magazine surmised, a sort of folk-hero in the West, any recollections really belonged to the public, especially to Linderman and Russell fans.*

The first reading of Linderman's writing showed me that he had expressed himself in tired language and inadequate form. A principal weakness was the constant use of participial phrases, which subordinated ideas or actions or feelings of both Russell and Linderman and weakened the dramatic effect that was characteristic of the writing and the storytelling of both men. My principal departure from the original writing has been the changing of many of these phrases and the bringing out, thereby, of dramatic effects.

The actual insertions of words or phrases or sentences have been few. Chiefly, they are words portraying typical actions of the men, such as "He rolled a cigarette," coming at a place when a pause seems profitable. Or they provide a transition or a time sequence when one seems needed, such as "After a few years" or "Once he told me." Short phrases or clauses such as "Before I could answer" add a touch which, narrative-wise, seem of interest. Such a sentence as "He turned to me" at times emphasizes what was going on both physically and mentally.

Two or three times an informative clause or sentence had to be added; for instance, where the manuscript read, "Fires at Lake McDonald called him [Russell] there," I wrote, "Fires at Lake McDonald, where his summer cabin was, called him there." Once in a great while, when from long-ago conversation with Frank I knew the strength of his opinion on a matter, I added an emphatic word or phrase; for instance, where the manuscript read, "It was this that caused the trouble [for Russell in painting a picture]," I wrote, "It was this and nothing else that caused the trouble." (Linderman had been asked, in this instance, to request Russell to paint something "that is standing still"; Russell acquiesced but could not make the buffalo bull stand still.) Again, at one place when Linder-man was looking at a Russell painting, Charley turned his back on him. Why? Explanation was needed; at the right place I added, "Now I knew why he had turned his back on me."

All of my additions were underscored on the draft which I submitted to the three Linderman daughters for their approval or disapproval. All told, the changes would add up to fill only a small space, and they have made the account more natural and readable.

These details of alteration are presented here to assure the reader that the manuscript is Frank Linderman's expression and that no incidents and no conversations and no descriptions have had violence done to them.

In the manuscript Linderman wrote, ". . . in telling of our days together I promise no sequence in the tales themselves." He also stated that dates were of no importance. It seemed to me, however, that the placing together of incidents of like nature would make the account more readily and clearly informative and interesting. For in-

stance, the three accounts of Russell's visits in the Goose Bay home bring out, when grouped, elements in Russell's nature not shown in incidents like the camping trips. Or again, the three accounts of Russell out of his habitat, when grouped, reveal more emphatically his attitude toward "civilized" society.

Lastly, I have written brief headnotes to the chapters, hoping to give the reader clarifying or interesting information, and by this means to lessen the number of necessary footnotes.

Frank Linderman always wrote "Charley"; I have used that spelling except when quoting from writers who wrote "Charlie."

Unless otherwise noted, all paintings, sculptures, and drawings reproduced herein are the work of Charles M. Russell, and are used through the courtesy of the Montana Historical Society, Helena.

I am indebted for help to my wife Doris; to the cooperation of the three Linderman daughters, without which the work could not have been undertaken, and *when undertaken could not have been finished; to Dr. Van Kirke Nelson of Kalispell, Montana, for permission to use pictures from his Western collection; to Michael Kennedy, of the Montana Historical Society, for encouragement and for use of Russell paintings. I also appreciate the shove toward the taking up of the task which J. Frank Dobie gave me.*

H. G. Merriam

Missoula, Montana

CONTENTS

ILLUSTRATIONS

RECOLLECTIONS OF
Charley Russell

Frank Bird Linderman and Charles M. Russell were friends for more than thirty years. Russell, the older man by five years, became for the younger man a sort of hero by virtue of his sturdy, unshakable Westernism. Both loved primitive country, the outdoor life, wild animals, and the early days when a man felt few social pressures and was his own boss. Both respected and, in his measure, understood the old Indian.

EVEN on the western slopes of the Rockies far
from his habitat I had in the eighties heard of Charley
Russell, the Paintin' Kid. I had seen pictures of his, then found
only in saloons, and they had captivated me as they had all men
who had lived in the unspoiled West. They were full of action
and in atmosphere were boisterous. My imagination built a
Russell corresponding to the features of the paintings. When
we met, soon after his marriage and when he was living in Great
Falls,[1] I saw a gentle man of medium height, neither stout nor
thin, with yellow hair and yellow eyes, and hands that drew
my attention. His manner was quiet. I was disappointed.

I could not, however, have mistaken his breeding, for his good
lineage was self-evident.[2] Born in St. Louis on March 19, 1864,
he had come to Montana Territory about the year 1881[3] and

[1] Charley Russell and Nancy Cooper were married on September 9, 1896.
[2] "The half-century old estate in the Oak Hill suburb [of St. Louis] where
the cowboy [Russell] spent his early boyhood was strongly reminiscent of a
colonial Virginia plantation. . . . The Russell family operated the most exten-
sive coal diggings in the region." Later, Russell's father became the president
of the Parker-Russell Mining and Manufacturing Company, which built "a
large plant to convert fire clay into tile and brick . . . gas works . . . rolling
mills." It was "the largest firm of its kind in the country." (McCracken, *op. cit.*,
22.) Charley's family tried hard to educate him and resisted his urge to go
west, but he did not like school and had heard too many tales from men who
had been clear up to Fort Benton, and his longing was not to be resisted.
"Through all his years of drifting [Russell] had never lost his air of being
to the manner born, no matter how disreputable his outward appearance
might be . . . [he] made friends with many fine men of the town [Great Falls]."
(Shelton, *op. cit.*, 119).
[3] Russell came to Montana early in March, 1880.

3

had cut himself off from his family. He never talked of his parents or of his boyhood in St. Louis. He was alone, making his own way. The life of the West so captured him that he determined to make himself thoroughly Western and quickly adopted the customs and the speech as he saw and heard them among his associates on the cattle range. He made them his own forever.

The West said, "Stand on your own feet." It allowed no questioning of a man's past, especially a stranger's. To do so was insulting. Charley Russell from the beginning stood on his own feet, asked no questions, and offered no hint of his past.

Charley was self-contained. He avoided arguments and strangers with as much care as an old Indian. Gentle though he was, his lips, chin, and jaws told anyone that he was no quitter and that, if crowded or cornered, he might even be dangerous. He was as full of pure grit as a badger. Yet if he had an enemy among men I never knew him.

Once he asked me, pertaining to nothing that had passed between us, "Ever pull a crooked deal?" The query was disarmingly sudden.

"Depends on what you mean by crooked deal," I said, looking at him sitting cross-legged on the other side of our lodge fire. "I've done things that I'd not square with my conscience," I admitted.

"I mean," he said, deliberately putting down a sketch he had been making in the firelight, "I mean, did you ever keep any money that didn't belong to you?"

4

the feller loosened up buyin' drinks. An' he was havin' a good time like we was.

"Money? He'd spent piles of it, kept me an' Bill stewed for two weeks. If he left the bar at all, even to eat or sleep, I didn't know about it. Finally, somebody told him I was a painter. Right away he takes me off to one side an' his eyes was as dead lookin' as a frozen coyote's. 'Mr. Russell,' he says, 'I want you to paint me two pictures while I'm here.' His hands showed me the size he was lookin' for. 'The work must be done and the pictures delivered to me here so I can take 'em home with me. Will you accept this commission, Mr. Russell?' he asks. He led me by the hand back to the bar for another drink.

"Wow! I left the bunch lickin' up booze an' pulled out for the cabin like somebody was after me with a butcher knife. I painted fast. I was afraid the feller's money would be all gone if I didn't hurry up. I didn't eat an' I didn't sleep till I had two pictures done. I let 'em dry while I filled up with grub an' slept the clock plumb around. They wasn't very dry when I packed 'em into the barroom of the old Park. An' there he was right where I'd left him, belly up against the bar with a crowd round him that made me think of magpies round a dead hoss. But I didn't wait, no sir! 'Here's your pictures, pardner,' I says, handin' 'em out an' steppin' back a little.

"He took 'em, holdin' the frame of one of 'em in his hand an' settin' the other up against the wall at the end of the bar. He walked off to look at it, squintin' like he knew somethin' about paintin'. Then he set the other one up, doin' the same way. The crowd was all eyes an' ears like I was. I plumb had to have that money.

" 'Excellent, excellent,' he says low like, like he was talkin' to himself. Then he shook my hand an' says, 'I like 'em, Mr. Russell. How much do I owe you, sir?'

"I got crooked as a coyote's hind leg. I says to myself. 'Here's where I throw the big harpoon into you an' turn it plumb around.' While the crowd pushes up to the pictures at the end of the bar I think some more. 'Fifty dollars!' I says, like I felt I was makin' up for the drinks he'd bought me. I'd have taken ten.

" 'Thank you,' he says, pullin' out a wad that'd plug a sewer. 'I shall always feel that I am in your debt, Mr. Russell,' he says an' peels off a hundred dollars an' hands 'em to me.

"Wow! I took it. Yes, sir, an' I kept it. You see, he thought I meant fifty dollars apiece for the pictures instead of for the two. I shoved the hundred into my pants pocket without battin' an eye. An' I kept it!

" 'Have a drink on me, pardner,' I says right quick, callin' up all the boys. An' then, by God, I high-tailed it for the cabin to hide out. He ain't seen me since."

"Well," I said to Charley, "I might have done something like that some time."

Charley merely grunted and reached for my rifle, which had caught his eye. He fondled it, turning it slowly in the firelight. "You're a dead-center gun an' a meat getter," he muttered to it. He held the rifle across his lap and rubbed its stock. "You roar like a cannon an' I bet ya kick like an army mule. Lemme cut some fresh meat on the old gal?" he asked across the fire.

8

I nodded and he opened the small blade of his jackknife.

I brightened the blaze with dry wood and went around the fire and sat beside him, watching the point of the blade bite into the steel of the rifle's frame without hesitation, without a slip, and make the "fresh meat"—a buffalo bull, a buffalo cow and calf, a bull elk, a mountain sheep, and a grizzly bear. They seemed to walk out of the metal as though pricked into life by the blade. "C.M.R.—1913," the knife recorded, and then his mark, a buffalo skull.

"There she is," he chuckled and handed me the rifle. "Now the old gal will always have fresh meat in sight."

The engraving was unbelievably fine, marvelous when one considered the light and the instrument used. The animals were so sharply cut into the steel that prints might easily be taken from them.

Unfortunately the rifle was not mine, had never been mine. It belonged to Montana's Territorial Governor, Sam T. Hauser of Helena. I had borrowed it several years before to go bear hunting and had never returned it because the Governor had asked me to keep it until he called for it. I knew that he would never want the rifle again, because his hunting days were over, but his son, Tom Hauser, might want it. I said nothing about this to Charley, who had given the rifle no particular attention until two years before when I had made a scratch shot that had surprised him. Now I was determined to get a clear title to the old gun. I succeeded the following spring.

"Have you father's bear rifle?" Tom Hauser asked, uncertainly.

"Yes. Want it?" I replied, wondering how to manage its purchase.

"Yes, I'm going to try for a bear next week."

"Should think it would be a little heavy for you, climbing mountains," I said.

" 'Tis," Tom admitted, "but it's the best I've got." He added in a moment, "It's got an awful wallop."

"You bet it has and at both ends," I laughed. Then I ventured, "Say, Tom, you go over to Holter's hardware store and pick out any rifle that pleases you and have them send me the bill. I love the old gun and I'd like to keep it. How about it?" I tried not to sound eager.

To my surprise, he agreed readily, and I have never paid a bill with more pleasure. The old gun is beside me now. I looked at it to get the date of Charley's engraving, which is as sharp and clear as ever. I think maybe I should have confessed to Charley that what I did might be as crooked as his keeping the hundred dollars for the pictures when he was asking only fifty, for Tom didn't know about Charley's engraving on the gun and I didn't tell him.

In his early days here in Montana, Charley was a boy among men who drank, so that from those days up to within seventeen years of his passing Charley drank, sometimes to excess. He never denied his love for whisky and never offered excuses for his sprees. At last, he realized that he could not both drink and paint, so he quit drinking.[5] After his decision he never touched

[5] Shelton, *op. cit.,* 182, states that he stopped drinking on an early promise to his wife. No doubt both Linderman and Shelton are right. "Nancy and

a drop of liquor. "It ain't because I've had all I want," he once told me, his jaws set like those of a closed vise, "but because I've had more than my share of booze."

Nobody among his close friends believed that he could cut off his drinking so suddenly, so abruptly, so completely as he did. Some of them thought that he had only discontinued patronizing saloons and was drinking secretly. They were wrong. Charley could not have done such a thing; he was too honest. Besides, he had had wide experience with liquor and knew what it could do to men.

When finally the cattle industry began to wane in the Northwest many cowpunchers, forced to find other employment, became sheriffs, deputy sheriffs, livery stablemen, and saloonkeepers in the old cow towns. Charley and a partner opened a gin mill in Chinook. This, of course, was before he had decided to stop drinking. He seldom spoke of this venture; his stories of it were rare. "Trouble was," he said to me, "we tried to drink it all up ourselves an' couldn't quite make it. But we did a pretty good job just the same. There wasn't much left but some Virginia Dare an' a little mineral water when they shut us up." He paused, "I don't remember makin' any money." He paused again, "Just the same, she was a mighty popular joint as long as she lasted."[6]

Charles had an understanding that when he was with the boys he was to take two drinks, no more. . . . When he left the house, the understood signal was two upraised fingers, meaning, 'Remember, no more than two drinks.' Upon his return, if he had broken over, he would signal the fact with the upraised fingers of his hand—or hands!" (Adams and Britzman, *op. cit.*, 150.)

[6] According to Shelton, this was in 1892 and Con Price was the partner.

Charley was extremely tolerant toward men who drank, remembering his own drinking and his battle to loosen liquor's grip upon him. When national prohibition came he was opposed to it. "I ain't like old John Mathewson," he declared. "You know yourself that John kept himself soused for more'n forty years, and then when the doctors told him he'd have to quit drinking or die he quit. But then right away he thought every man that took a drink ought to be hung. I ain't goin' to let myself get like that.

"Prohibition!" he would say, with his inimitable chuckle, "We're the biggest fools on earth. 'Twas bad enough when men met an' visited an' drank in decent saloons in daylight. Now, under this fool law, men drink in the dark, an' behind garbage cans in alleys, an' plumb alone. I see 'em makin' their sneaks with poison stuff they buy from bootleggers. An' anyway, this drinkin' alone is mighty bad medicine."

Not once did I hear him mention his struggle against liquor. It must at first have required all his strong will. He must have been tempted often, even as I myself once unwittingly tempted him. Yet he held firmly to his resolution to let drink alone.

We were hunting elk together. The day had been stormy, with rain and sleet, and we were wet to our skins. Reaching our lodge, chilled to the bone, I hastily started a fire, set a tin cup of water

---

When they opened for business, friends filed in but "nobody ordered a drink, so the proprietors started the ball rolling by 'settin' 'em up' for the house. The ball started rolling, all right, but everyone who ordered a drink said airily, 'just charge it.' . . . In a few days, their friends had literally drunk them out of business."

on it, and dropped in a little sugar. I took a pint bottle of bourbon whisky from my war bag and poured a decent drink of it into the cup, that was now hot.

"Lemme smell it," Charley said eagerly as I took up the steaming toddy.

"Keep it, I'll make another," I told him, knowing that he was even more thoroughly chilled than I.

He smelled the liquor, sniffing it as one smells a flower. "God," he said sorrowfully, "if I could only drink whisky like you can I'd give a leg. But I can't. If I took that drink I'd fight you for the bottle." He returned the cup to me untasted.

After that, wet or dry, warm or cold, I never took liquor on our hunting trips.

Freed from liquor, Charley became marvelously regular in his habits. He rose before sunup winter and summer, cooked his breakfast, built a fire in his studio when the weather was cold, and began work early. He painted until noon. After the midday meal he stretched himself upon a couch to nap for thirty minutes, snoring lustily. His nap finished, he returned to the studio to work a while longer before going downtown to visit with friends until five o'clock.

One could be nearly certain to find Charley any day by walking down Main Street in Great Falls during late afternoon. His horse, Monte, stood in front of some place of business and marked his hangout. When death from old age took Monte to the Shadow Hills, Charley's visits to town lost much of their glamor— "There wasn't any good place for old Monte to wait for me downtown any more," he said sadly.

Fame came to Charley but it found no fawning in him. If he recognized its coming, he denied acquaintance; he never admitted that it had favored him or that it had ever heard of him. He heartily disliked having his fame mentioned. Men who pretended acquaintance with him—and they were many—had his sorrowful abomination. They also amused him. One rainy day we were on a train from Helena to Great Falls. When we chose our seats the half-dozen passengers in the coach were far apart. The train entered a tunnel, and puffs of acrid smoke came in through an open transom above the seat ahead of us. A dapper man of about forty years, a passenger from across the aisle, moved over and closed the transom with a satisfying snap. To close it he had stood upon the seat, and when the train flashed out of the tunnel he was sitting there. He turned to look into our faces as if seeking approbation. "Thanks," I said.

But the man was talkative. "I'd like to stop off in Great Falls and have a visit with Charley Russell, the famous cowboy artist, but I can't spare the time." He looked regretfully out of the rain-streaked window.

"Do you know Russell?" I asked. I felt Charley beginning to squirm in the seat beside me.

"Oh my, yes. We went to school together in St. Louis when we were children. We were chums. Bright boy, Charley was."

"That must have been 'way back in the nineties. Well, he'd be glad to see you, I'm sure." Charley kicked my foot.

"Are you acquainted with him?" the man asked, as though suddenly sensing possibilities.

"I've seen him," I replied.

14

I knew that the answer would clear the trail for the fellow's further lying. But Charley put an end to the entertainment. "Come on, I want a smoke," he said, leading the way to the smoker. He was thoroughly disgusted. "Hell of a lot of schoolin' he got if he went to school with me, the damned dirty liar. Went to school with me," he growled, amazed at the man's cheek. "Humph! Why, he ain't dry behind the ears yet."

*Every Russell fan knows of the two formative
years, his seventeenth and eighteenth, which Charley spent
with Jake Hoover, a genuine old-time mountain man, in
his cabin in Pig-Eye Basin on the South Fork of the Judith
River. He was living in a country brand new to him that
abounded in wild life and was associated with a type of
man he may have dreamed about but had never intimately
known. Russell students realize that Jake molded Charley
into the Western man he became.*[1]

*The tale of "Jake Hoover's Pig" has been current folk-
lore for many a year. I heard it first about 1916 from John
R. Barrows, author of* Ubet *and for one short period a
cowboy working with Charley. Since then I have heard
it variously told by other persons. I don't know who first
communicated it from Russell's telling, but Frank Linderman told it, in almost the words used here, in his collec-*

---

[1] A good account of Jake's meeting with Charley is in McCracken, *op. cit.,*
46–53. It is also told well in Shelton, *op. cit.,* and briefly in Adams and Britzman, *op. cit.;* of course Nancy Russell tells it in her biographical note in *Good
Medicine,* and Austin Russell, *op. cit.,* mentions it. On page 33, Shelton writes:
Jake "became fond of Charlie and took great pleasure in helping mold the
boy into the fine man he wanted him to become." This probably flatters Jake's
ambition for Charley. Charley returned again and again to the Hoover cabin,
sometimes for fairly long stays; it was his home before his marriage. McCracken
writes, on page 93, that Jake "always encouraged his [Charley's] drawing
and modeling."

tion of Western tales entitled On a Passing Frontier *(1920).*
The story is told by Shelton and by Adams and Britzman.

"The Ivory-handled Six-shooter" is also something of
a folk tale. It too I first heard from John R. Barrows,
whose father and mother ran the Stagecoach Hotel and
Bar at Ubet in the Judith Basin, where the east-west and
the north-south routes met in the early eighties. It is more
traditional than the tale of Jake Hoover and his pig in that
the trading of firearms and one trader's getting the better
of the other and then passing on the bad deal was a thing
that was constantly experienced by cowboys. Such tales
acquired status and stature with each telling.

Any equipment that was colorful and showy was valued
by the old-time cowboy. A six-shooter with a pearl or ivory
handle drew immediate admiration wherever it was seen.
Inevitably someone would want to try shooting it.

"Jake Hoover's Pig"

"THEY was funny old boys, them fellers," Charley said, thoughtfully, referring to the old-time trappers. "They had a lot of sentiment an' didn't know it. Of course, a man don't look for much sentiment in a trapper—I mean when it comes to killin' an animal." He rolled a cigaret, lighted it, and inhaled a puff of smoke. "But sometimes it's there just the same."

I knew when Charley had a story coming and waited.

"When I was a kid I threw in with old Jake Hoover. Jake was a trapper an' a skin hunter an' killed deer an' antelope an' elk for the market for fresh meat. He did a lot of things that was ornery. His cabin was in Pig-Eye Basin over in Judith country. You could see deer from the door of his shack 'most any day. But do you think he would kill a deer that stuck about his shack? No, sir, he'd as soon take a shot at men as kill one of them deer. An' I've seen the time when there wasn't enough grub in that shack to bait a mousetrap, too. Every livin' thing around there liked old Jake. Pine squirrels would climb into his lap an' sit on his shoulder. Chickadees were dead stuck on him; they'd pick crumbs from his lips an' he always fed 'em plenty.

"One spring a ranchman in the Judith traded old Jake a little suckin' pig for some elk meat. He was tiny, black as ink, an' cute as a kit fox. Jake chucked him into a gunny sack, tied it behind his saddle, an' fetched the pig to the cabin in Pig-Eye Basin, turnin' him loose there. Inside of two days that little pig was follerin' old Jake wherever he went, up hill and down again, just like a dog. He got to be an awful nuisance. We couldn't keep him out of the cabin, an' he was into everythin' that smelled like grub. He even wanted to sleep with us—got sore as a wolf when we wouldn't let him. So we built a pen for him an' shut him up.

"Wheat was scarce in those days. We had to rustle hard to feed that pig. We always had to find ranchmen who'd rather have elk meat than wheat, because we didn't have any money. But shuttin' that pig up was good for him; he seemed to swell up overnight.

"Jake was dead stuck on that pig. He made a reg'lar ceremony of feedin' him, too. Soon's he'd step into the pen with grub in a camp kettle the pig would rub Jake's shins with his snout, an' the old man would lean over an' scratch the pig's back, talkin' all the time. " 'Ain't he a dandy, kid?' he'd say when I was around. 'Won't he make fine eatin' this fall, hey? By God, I'm glad I got him. A man's a damn fool that don't have a pig in these here hills. I ain't never goin' to be without one any more, you bet.' Then he'd empty the kettle into the wooden trough an' say, 'There, eat, you damned glutton. Git good an' fat, 'cause when fall comes we'll smash ya a good lick atween yer eyes with the ax. Then we'll have grease till grass starts in the spring. Lucky we got ya.'

"One mornin' we went huntin' an' was gone three days. When we come back an' was comin down a steep pitch that was near the cabin we heard a tin pan go 'bang' inside it. 'Hold on, kid,' Jake says, cockin' his rifle. 'There's a bear in the shack an' he might be a grizzly. Take keer of yaself.'

"I was lookin' over his shoulder when he poked the muzzle of his Winchester through the open door. But it wasn't a bear;

the pig had got out of his pen an' got into the cabin. The place was always tidy, but now it was the damndest wreck in Montana Territory. The pig had found Jake's flour an' molasses an' dried apples an' rolled 'em up plenty in a mess. Molasses an' flour was plastered over everythin'. Worse'n all, he'd dragged old Jake's four-point Hudson's Bay blanket off'n the bunk an' had walloped it round in the mess. You remember them old-fashioned dried apples that used to come in round slices with round holes in the middle? Well, one of them slices had stuck fast to the pig's forehead, an' I bet every fly in the Territory had moved in an' camped on the sticky spots on Jake's blanket.

"He was a pig, remember; but snortin' an' blowin' an' rollin' in the flour an' molasses had made rings round his eyes like he had goggles on, an' the slice of apple stuck on his forehead was the funniest thing I ever saw.

"He was tickled to death to see us an' showed it plain; but old Jake was mad clean to his toes. 'This settles it with you, ya damned dirty rooter,' he said, kickin' the pig in the ribs as he went through the door. 'Ya won't see no leaves turn yellow; you'll be bacon. Good God, just look at my blanket, kid,' he says, draggin' it outdoors.

"I wanted to laugh but I was afraid to. I helped clean up the mess without sayin' anythin', but Old Jake was swearin' like a stuck bullwhacker all the time.

"Soon's we had supper old Jake started to sharpen butcher knives. I didn't know he had so many knives. I went to sleep hearin' 'em grit on his whetstone. I felt sorry for the pig.

"At daylight I turned out an' put on my boots. 'Hold on, kid,'

Jake says, sittin' up in his bunk. 'It's too warm to kill that pig in this weather, it's too warm; the meat would spoil an' we don't wanta lose it after all the hell we've had with him. Besides, there's some wheat left an' we wouldn't have nothin' to feed it to. We'll wait a spell.'

"I was glad. I liked that fool pig.

"The wheat didn't last long; we had to make another rustle. 'It's the last time, kid,' Jake said. 'I'm plumb sick of the contract. Soon's this sack's gone, zowie! We'll bat him a good one with the ax.' He looked both fierce an' a bit sad. 'It's comin' to him, ain't it?'

" 'Sure is,' I agreed, though I was mighty glad we had another big sack of wheat, just the same.

"The weather was growin' sharp when the last of our wheat was dished out. 'In the mornin' we'll kill him,' Jake said. 'I'll feed him tonight an' bust his damned dirty head in the mornin',' he growled, sharpening butcher knives again.

"At daylight he called, 'Come on, roll out, kid. We'll git rid of that low-down skunk afore we eat. I jest can't put it off any longer. I been layin' there in my bunk thinkin' of that blanket he ruined. An' besides, the wheat's all gone an' I ain't goin' ridin' like a madman to find feed for a damned hawg no more. Come on, roll out.' He picked up a handful of butcher knives an' the camp kettle he'd always used to feed the pig. 'Fetch the ax,' he says like he was mad at me.

"We started for the pigpen. A pine squirrel came down a fir tree an' up the trail to meet us, but old Jake kicked him. An' when a chickadee lit on his shoulder the old feller dropped his

21

camp kettle, snatched off his hat, an' struck at the little bird with it. 'Kid,' he says, 'this gulch is plumb overrun with damn nuisances. It's got so a man can't live here no more. I know what I'll do; by God, I'll move out an' let 'em have it.'

"The pig was tickled to see Jake. He rubbed his snout against Jake's shins as soon's he stepped into the pen. 'Git away from here, damn ya. Ya think this is a friendly visit? Well, it ain't. Here, kid,' he says, handing me the ax, 'smash him a good one while I git the water heatin'.'

" 'Not by a damn sight; he ain't my pig,' I said to Jake, backing away.

" 'Oh, come on, kid; he's knowed me ever since he was a little feller. The wheat's all gone and we need the meat.'

" 'Can't help it,' I said, 'I didn't bring him here an' I won't kill him.'

" 'No, but you'll eat his meat fast enough, I bet,' Jake growled. He leaned the ax against the pen.

" 'Well, I won't kill him, that's a cinch,' I said an' climbed out of the pen.

"Old Jake quit me cold an' went back to the cabin mutterin' to himself, mad as a hornet. I saw him come out with his rifle an' start up the hill. He climbed until the timber hid him. The pig all the time was watching me, waitin' for somethin' to eat.

"I fed him an' he nosed round in the empty kettle an' then looked around for Jake.

"Bang! I jumped a foot high an' the pig tumbled over an' began to kick beside the kettle.

"Old Jake came down off the hill, leaned his rifle against the pen, pulled out a butcher knife, an' stuck the pig. I can see him yet ashakin' the blood off the knife.

" 'I don't reckon he saw me or knowed who done it, do you, kid?' he asks, lookin sorry as a woman."

"The Ivory-handled Six-shooter"

ONE MORNING when I was in Charley's studio I pulled an old ivory-handled six-shooter from its holster. He had carved a steer's head in the ivory, and the passing years had enriched the coloring. I tried the gun's lock, having always liked to hear the click of the old Colt. The hammer wouldn't stand cocked; the dog had been worn away.

"That gun has seen better days," I said, idly returning it to the holster on the wall.

"She sure has," Charley replied. He squatted in a hard-bottomed kitchen chair before his easel. "Did I ever tell you how I got her? No? Well, it was one of the crookedest deals I ever made. I was a kid then." He stepped down from the chair, chuckling, and put his palette and brushes on it. He lighted a cigaret.

"My brother an' another feller was camped in Judith Basin. I was wranglin' hosses for the Bear Paw Pool outfit. Our wagons wasn't far from where my brother[2] was hangin' out, so one mornin' I saddled a hoss an' rode over to see him.

"There was nobody around the cabin when I got there. Its door was wide open, so I went in to size things up. Hangin' on

[2] Charley's younger brother Ed came to Montana after Charley's first visit to St. Louis.

an antelope's horn that was stuck in the wall I saw a six-shooter in a brand new holster. The bright sunlight that streamed through the door landed full on the six-shooter's butt, an' it was made of mother-of-pearl. All the colors of a fine fire-opal was jiggin' an' glancin' on it. Wow! I was stuck for keeps.

"Nobody was in sight when I looked out the door so I pulled the gun from its holster. Wow! It was silver plated, the barrel was chased with a vine of gold leaves on both sides, an' every chamber of the cylinder had a little vine of gold leaves. I balanced it in my hand, fondled it, an' itched to own it myself.

"I heard a hoss comin' an' got cunnin'. I chucked the gun back in its holster an' started for the door. In comes my brother.

" 'How!' he says. 'Where'd ya came from?'

" 'Just rode over from the wagon. Been here quite a while. Some shack ya got.'

" 'Yeah,' he says right short.

" 'Got a new gun, I see.'

" 'Yeah.'

"I looked at the six-shooter like I hadn't seen it before. 'Some butt on it,' I says, careless as I could. I took it from its holster an' handled it an' then dropped it back in. 'Where'd ya get her?'

" 'Sent back to the States for her last month. Hungry?' he asks.

" 'Yep.'

" 'I'll cook ya something,' he says, goin' into a little lean-to that had a stove in it.

"I followed him. 'How'll ya trade guns?' I was itchin' all over.

" 'What ya got?' he asks, cuttin' a steak from the ham of an antelope an' layin' it on the table.

24

"I had just bought a good Colt forty-five. She was blued an' clean as a wolf's tooth. 'She's brand new an' a dead-center,' I says, braggin'.

"He shoved his gun across the table an' cut another steak. 'Oh, I don't know,' he says, like a father that's thinkin' of givin' somethin' to his youngest kid. 'My gun's a lot of trouble—all fancy; gotta keep shinin' her all the time. You're a kid an' like to caper round the gals.' He stopped workin' on the steak an' looked at me, 'If you're dead stuck on my gun, I'll trade ya even up.' He put the meat in the fryin' pan an' salted it. He hadn't even looked at my gun.

"Even up! Wow! I changed holsters so quick I got the new one on my belt wrong side to.

"My brother stirred up the fire an' I started for the door to try my new gun. There was a tomato can with a big red tomato on it about twenty-five yards from the shack, a bully target. I stood in the door an' used both hands to give the gun the best of it an' pulled down on that red tomato. Bow! My God, if it hadn't been for the top of that door frame that gun would have split my skull wide open. Roar? My ears was ringin' like church bells. Hit the can? Hell, no; I didn't even hit Judith Basin.

"I looked at the gun. One side was all smoky. I tried to cock the damn thing an' couldn't; the cylinder wouldn't turn. It couldn't 'cause a shavin' of lead as thick's a slice of bread was wedged in between it an' the barrel. They didn't line up, didn't track. Bullets had to round a corner to get out. An' every bullet that left that gun was a cripple, a half-bullet. But nothin' would be in danger from the gun except the man that pulled the trigger.

"I was stuck good an' plenty but I didn't let on. I poked my fool gun into my holster an' went to the door of the lean-to where my brother was fryin' the meat. He was grinnin'; mebby he was laughin' out loud. I couldn't 'uv heard him if he was. 'Guess I'll be ridin',' I says. My voice sounded as if it was down a well.

" 'Ain't ya goin' to eat?' he asks—or I thought he says somethin' like that.

" 'Nope,' I says, an' I pulled out right away. I didn't even look back.

"By an' by my hoss flushed a covey of prairie chickens. I'd been worryin' about my ears, but I heard them chickens cluck when they flew away an' I was tickled plenty. Pretty soon I got so's I could hear meadow larks.

"In the Gap[3] I saw a rider comin'. It was Bill Deaton. Right away I figgered on tradin' guns with Bill. Bill always had a good outfit, from saddles to spurs. When I got near I dug my spurs into my hoss so's he would dance and get the sunlight caperin' on the butt of my gun.

" 'Hello, Kid. God Almighty, that's a pretty barker ya got there. Lemme see her,' he says, pullin' up beside me.

"I handed her out an' I was mighty glad I'd rubbed the smoke off her.

" 'Man, she's fancy, ain't she? Where'd ya get her?'

"I thought if my brother's yarn was strong enough to hook me it might tangle Bill, too, so I said, 'Oh, I sent back to the States for her last month.'

---

[3] Judith Gap in central Montana.

" 'Pretty gun; damned pretty gun,' he says, 'pretty's a white-faced calf. Yes, sir.' he says, balancin' my six-shooter in his hand. 'By God, that butt would make jewelry, wouldn't it, Kid, jewelry for a lady, hey?'

" 'Sure would,' I says. But I didn't tell him that was all 'twas good for.

" 'How'll ya trade, Kid?'

" 'Oh, I don't know. What ya got?' I rolled me a cigaret like I didn't care a damn.

" 'This,' he says, handing out that gun you just looked at. She was as good as they made 'em.

" 'Well,' I says, 'I'm gettin' sick of polishing my gun. She's pretty fancy. You always have a rattlin' fine outfit an' ya like to shine round the gals a lot. If you're dead stuck on my gun, I'll trade even up.' I spoke like it didn't make any difference to me.

"Wow! You'd 'a thought my gun was a fly an' old Bill was a speckled trout the way he grabbed that trade. If you think I loafed around there, you're fooled. I drifted right now! I was on top of a knoll when I heard, Bow! Bill was tryin' his new gun. I lifted my hoss up off the ground with my spurs an' held him there, touchin' nothin' but the high spots all the rest of the way to the wagons.

"I didn't see old Bill again till the fall round-up. He was reppin' for an outside iron an' was with our wagons.[4] Neither

---

[4] The "rep" or "outside man" represented his brand (iron) during general roundups. He examined brands on cattle rounded up and had those bearing his employer's brand separated out. He had to know brands and earmarks thoroughly.

27

of us mentioned our gun trade. Both of us had different reasons for lettin' it alone.

"One night when me an' him was alone by our chuck-wagon fire I let my curiosity get the best of me. 'Did ya ever shoot that gun I traded ya, Bill?' I was sorry the minute I spoke.

" 'Once, Kid, jest once. She knocked me an' my hoss down flat; yessir, flat!'

" 'What'd ya do with her?' I asked, seeing he wasn't very sore.

" 'Jest what you did, you dirty damn crook, an' I been hidin' out ever since.' "

*Self-portrait, showing Charley Russell dressed in his
invariable red sash, boots, and hat, in 1900.*

From the Britzman Collection
Courtesy of Hammer Galleries, New York

To Frank B. Linderman
with my best wishes   Carl Link
Goosebay, Sept. 2nd 1937

Frank Bird Linderman, drawn by Carl Link at Goose Bay.

Courtesy of Norma Linderman Waller

Charley and Nancy Russell, soon after their marriage.

Charley Russell posed in Indian garb, before his sojourn with the Bloods in 1888.

In camp a man throws off the restraints of every day, and his spirit flows out toward freedom until he begins to feel and act himself. Charley and Frank reveled in such days and often went camping together. They opened out to one another, telling tales, swapping reminiscences, laughing together, having an all-around good time. These camping trips, however, were for both men more than play; they were renewal of comradeship, of a loved way of living, of refreshment of spirit.

AN exchange of letters had set a date for Charley and me to meet at his studio and go camping. When I arrived at his studio, a log cabin which he called "the shack," he was busily painting. "Ho! Ho! Hi-eeeeeeee," he called out as he saw me enter, snatching away a brush held crosswise between his lips. His voice was as deep as an old Cree's. It was his usual greeting. With the grace of an Indian woman he signed for me to be seated, the rings on his fingers shining beneath the skylight.

I reflected that nothing pleased him more than to be mistaken for an Indian. Once he had donned a wig and dressed in a buckskin shirt, leggings, and moccasins and had his picture taken.[1] He had shown me the picture and asked, "Know this Injin?" "Yes," I said, instantly. But he saw that I was puzzled. "What's his name?" he pressed me. His yellow eyes betrayed his eagerness. "Running Antelope," I said, giving him his Pikuni name. His chagrin at my recognition made me wish that I had said, "No, who is it?"

"How's the missus an' the gals?" he asked. He put aside palette and brushes and rolled a cigarette.

I told him they were well and gave him their greetings.

"Ain't been doin' much," he said, showing me the pictures he had painted since my last visit. He seemed not to hear my

[1] Phil Weinhard and Charley, before going north to the Blood Indians in Canada, "outfitted themselves in Indian masquerade and went to the local photographer [in Helena] to have their picture taken—Weinhard as a stern buck and Charlie as his weak squaw." See Adams and Britzman, *op. cit.,* 92; the picture is on page 90. See also Shelton, *op. cit.,* 95.

praise as I looked at them one by one. He always pretended not
to hear it. Sometimes he asked me to name his pictures, but
when I did he seldom adopted my suggestions.

"Say, Frank," he went on, turning to his easel, "you've always
picked our huntin' trips. Lemme pick this one, hey?"

"Shoot, partner," I agreed, not caring where we went.

"South Fork of the Judith.[2] An' we'll go in from Neihart."
This came out so quickly that I knew he had been thinking of
it for some time, and was wishing to renew acquaintance with
the old mining camp on our way in. "I ain't been on the South
Fork of the Judith since I was a kid," he half muttered, as if to
cover his eagerness. He removed the unfinished picture from the
easel and leaned it against a wall. His eyes swept the cabin as
though he were wishing it good-bye. "Ho," he exclaimed and
slapped his lean hands together like an old Indian, "Ho!
Let's go!"

We checked our saddles, Indian lodge, and camp equipment
to Neihart at the station and were off. We expected to buy our
grub and hire horses at Neihart. When we tried to find horses
we found that they were scarce in the old camp. But we finally
got two cayuses for riding, and Charley secured a whopping big
Clydesdale for a pack animal.

The Clydesdale was not more than five years old, was as
gentle as a kitten, and had never carried a saddle or a pack.
"Whoa, pony," Charley said, stopping the big beast beside our
outfit in front of the general store. He chuckled, "When he walks
the world jiggles a little, but that won't hurt." He patted the

---

[2] This was where the Hoover cabin was.

horse's neck. "Old man Schlitz or some of them big brewers ought to have had him for their beer wagons." He added, "His owner's a house painter; maybe we can borrow a ladder from him." He laughed as he went on his toes to spread a saddle blanket on the big fellow's back.

We blindfolded the Clydesdale, took up a leg, and by standing on a dry-goods box borrowed from the storekeeper packed him without any trouble. However, we expected that as soon as his blind was removed and his leg let down, he would lie down and roll and we would have to do the packing all over. But he didn't.

"Let's drift," I suggested, swinging onto my cayuse and heading up the trail.

"You go ahead," Charley called, "I want to see a feller an' make a sketch."

I left him squatted in front of the store talking to a half-blood.

I had seen horses that could walk, but none that equaled our pack animal. The big horse strode like an elephant and set the pace. My cayuse trotted to keep ahead.

The morning was clear; the trail over a spur of the Little Belt Mountains steep. We were soon climbing, the big horse all but stepping on the heels of my pony. The lead rope on the Clydesdale was never taut as we went up and up. My pony scrambled until we reached the summit, a long, windy, nearly level hogback, with patches of snow along the trail. The level stretch inspired the big fellow. He let out another notch of his walking speed that made me marvel. I could now see the treetops pricking up from the Judith side of the Little Belts. "We'll be going downhill now," I thought. Then, without any warning whatever, the lead rope was jerked from my hands. I turned in the saddle and saw the big horse fall in a heap on the windy trail.

"He will roll and smash Charley's paint box," I thought, alarmed. I swung from the saddle and put my knee on the big fellow's neck, turning his heavy muzzle toward the sky. But again, he did not roll. Did not move. Did not seem even to breathe. "What's wrong," I wondered, and let the big head fall to the ground. Puzzled, I stuck my finger against his staring eye. The horse was as dead as a doornail!

I stood and looked along the trail. I saw Charley coming. He spurred his horse as I beckoned.

"What the hell's goin' on?" he shouted, pulling up beside me.

"We've got bear bait for a deadfall," I said.

We noticed that the horse was lying on his nigh side, so that we could get at neither the tie in the lash-rope nor the saddle's latigo.

"Wow!" Charley shot out, "What'll that baby cost us!" He got down and walked slowly about the animal, his thumbs hooked into his red sash.

I had already done my share of shivering about the cost of the horse. "Don't know," I said, "but there's no chance to dicker and the owner's got the edge." I drew my butcher knife and cut the lash-rope.

"Damned if I couldn't 'uv packed all he's got on him myself," Charley exclaimed disgustedly.

We pushed the light pack from the horse's back and salvaged the saddle.

33

"Better take his headstall, too," Charley advised. "Mebbe we'll need everything we can rustle to pay lawyers before we get a clear title to this carrion." He looked at me loweringly. "Now, damn it, we'll have to pack our ridin' hosses an' walk." He pitched the headstall violently at the pack.

Walking in his high-heeled riding boots had no charm for Charley, and yet he would wear nothing else on his feet. "Say, the Lost Fork of the Judith is a lot nearer than the South Fork, an' it's mighty good huntin' country, too. We can make for . . . By God, that hoss is breathing; I saw him." Charley snatched up the headstall. He hurried toward the Clydesdale, which was now staggering to his ponderous feet, shouting, "Whoa, whoa, whoa, boy! Whoa!"

But the big horse did not stop, didn't even falter. After one quick, dazed look at the landscape he headed away on the back trail, and he wasn't walking! But his tail was up, thank goodness.

"Why you dirty quitter!" Charley laughed, darting toward his pony.

"Stop!" I called. "Let that dirty devil go. I've never been so glad to see the southeast end of a horse going northwest in my life. Let him go."

We never saw him again. He must have reached his owner or we should have heard from him during the twenty-five years which have intervened.

We walked. In the afternoon we pitched our lodge in a pretty park on the Lost Fork. We had venison for supper, a young mule deer, fat as butter. Charley liked his meat fresh, the fresher the better.

34

"What the hell coulda been wrong with that fool hoss?" he wondered, over our lodge fire.

"Altitude, I guess." I added, "He was too ambitious; he was walking on my pony's heels."

"I'll take the cayuses for mine," he mused. "They've been here a long time. Altitude to a cayuse is like a preacher's sermon to old Frank Lampman, just a blank cartridge."

In two weeks we had eaten most of the young buck. As I wished to take home some venison, I began hunting again. Each day I saw only does until only one day of our trip was left. On the last day I still believed that I would find a buck and let several does go by, but when night came I had killed no meat.

Afoot and leading my cayuse I cut across the country for camp under a bright full moon that flooded the country. When I entered a long meadow not far from our lodge I saw a half-dozen white rumps go bounding into the skirting timber. I took a hasty shot at one of them as it disappeared into the shadows. I stood perfectly still, eyes and ears straining, but saw nothing that moved, heard nothing, except the report of my rifle echoing among the hills. "Missed," I thought. I walked to the spot where I had seen the white rump and nearly stumbled over an immense mule-deer doe. My shot had gone through her head. She had melted so suddenly in her tracks that I had not seen her fall. Dressing her was the work of only a few minutes, but loading her onto the horse required some time, because of her size. I had to use my rope, the saddle horn, and the limb of a tree to hoist her onto the pony.

The trail out of the meadow climbed a ridge that would lead

35

me high above our camp; the descent would be difficult because of its steepness, and I was tired. But when I saw the lodge among the dark trees below me in its firelit and moonlit whiteness, mottled with leaf shadows stirring in the night breeze, eeriness came upon me and rested me.

Charley was singing "Injin," in his high-pitched voice so perfectly imitating a red man's that if I had not known him to be alone in the lodge I might have been deceived.

I was as hungry as a wolf and yet I took great pleasure in the sight and the sound. The cayuse and I slid part of the way down the pitch, loosening stones that bounded noisily ahead of us. Charley heard nothing. Even when I let the heavy deer fall to the half-frozen ground near the lodge and hobbled my horse and turned him loose to find his mate, Charley's song continued.

I entered the lodge. He was singing in the firelight, beating the bottom of a grimy camp kettle with a stick which he had muffled with the dishrag. Eight small trout were laid out two by two before him on a finically folded pack mantle.

"Singing to them, Russ?" I asked, casually.

"Uh-huh," he replied without embarrassment. "That's the most fish I ever caught in my life. Wow! I wish you coulda seen 'em when I yanked 'em out of the water. They was sure awful pretty before their colors faded."

"Yeah," I said, picking up soap and a towel to go to the creek.

"I figured you was goin' to lay out all night," he said, setting the coffee pot on the lodge fire.

As I walked to the creek I tried again, as I had many times, to reconcile Charley's often-expressed belief in the orthodox

Christian religion with his adaptations of Indian pantheism. He sincerely believed that the whale swallowed Jonah, and mention of man's possible evolution from apelike creatures disgusted him. For atheist, heretic, agnostic, infidel, freethinker he had synonymous definitions, and any attempt to correct him was a waste of breath. "I notice that when these smart fellows come to the big ford," he would say, "they all quit like steers in a road." He truly believed that all who had dared question anything in Holy Writ recanted on their deathbeds—"if they possessed the breath," he would add. And yet, with all of this, he believed that the old-time Indian was right in his pantheism, especially in his reverence for the sun. And no Indian was a greater fatalist than he.

In October of 1910 or 1911 we hunted in the Swan Lake country. Our lodge was pitched on the site of an old trapping camp that had been mine in the eighties. Its dim evidences of earlier occupancy reminded me of many incidents. They amused Charley, particularly the ones dealing with my partner of those days, Black George. George was a white man, a Yankee, and reputedly a bad-man. He was a gun fighter who, when drunk, boasted of many killings, remembering and telling the gory details of each one. He was a crank, too. And yet, strangely enough, he was truthful. I never doubted his often-repeated boast that he had "drinked enough whisky to float a keelboat an' shot enough lead into buffalo to sink a man-o-war."

"Wow!" Charley would say as I told a story showing his hardness, "Did ya ever get into a bad wrangle with him?" He chuckled as he waited for my response.

37

"Well, our only quarrel flared when I tried to kill a tribe of deer mice that had built a nest of goose feathers in our supply of flour."

Charley laughed. "Yeah?" he said, bidding for more.

"We came close to a bad wrangle once," I said. "I had run my trap line. It was a cold day. I cut across the country for camp and met Black George on his line. He had but two traps yet to look at, so I fell in behind him to keep him company. We kept our trap lines tramped down, so that we could easily follow them wearing moccasins. But the night before this run there had been a heavy fall of snow, so that today we were on snowshoes.

"The last trap had a big lynx. George stepped out of his shoes and struck the lynx a blow on the head with his rifle barrel. 'I'll pack him into camp an' skin 'im out when I please,' he announced. He tied the big cat's near front paw to his off hind paw with a buckskin thong, making a loop of the animal's legs. He handed me his hat and rifle and lifted the lynx high. 'Buster, ain't he,' he laughed, sticking his head through the furry loop. The cat's body hung on his left side at his hips with two paws untied. 'All set,' he said, putting on his hat and taking his rifle.

"We had had a good day, for both of us had taken several pieces of fur. George was in a jolly mood, talking steadily as he swung along happily on his snowshoes. But the lynx wasn't dead. The blow on its head had only stunned it, and being jogged up and down at Black George's side revived it. If its head had been toward me instead of its tail, I might have noticed signs of trouble in time to warn my partner. Suddenly George's hat went sailing into a fir thicket. The action of the next few minutes was the wildest, most frantic I ever witnessed. The speed of it made details difficult to see. The crazed lynx clawed and scratched at Black George with its untied feet and spat at him. Black George was swearing strange oaths and trying to rid himself of the beast. All was a blinding whirl of fur and snow.

" 'Kill him, you damned fool! What the hell ya laughing at? Wanta see a man gutted?' He finally got the beast unloaded. His face, breast, arms, and hands were bloody.

"I felt ashamed of having laughed at the tussle that was so dangerous, and a bit skittish, too. I shot the hobbled lynx after a chase and later recovered George's rifle from the deep snow.

"When we reached camp I helped George remove his buckskin shirt. It's front and left side were in ribbons, cut as though by a sharp knife. Probably its toughness had saved George's life. At his direction I freely applied turpentine, his favorite medicine, to his raw wounds. It's the best thing I know when wounds are fresh. But the pain . . ."

"Wow!" said Charley.

" 'I reckon it did look funny,' Black George said, as our camp began to smell like a paint shop. 'I don't blame ya for laughin', son—not now, anyhow. But take this as a warnin', don't ya ever take one o' them devils out of a trap till ya know he's good and dead. Their toenails can raise more hell with a man than a butcher knife can.' George stretched his long body on his bunk. We both recalled the incidents of the struggle until we fell asleep."

"But just the same," Charley queried, "ornery as he was, he wouldn't let you kill the mice?" He stirred the lodge fire, chuckling. "What became of him?"

"I don't know," I said. "We split the blanket[3] at the head of this river the following summer, and I haven't seen him since. He might well be dead now."

"They was funny old boys, them fellers," Charley said, thoughtfully. "They had a lot of sentiment an' didn't know it."

Charley himself was steeped in sentiment, but he seldom expressed it except by a peculiar clearing of his throat, which his friends recognized for what it was.

One autumn when we were at Goose Bay, Charley and I loaded our Indian lodge and camp equipment into my car and drove through the forest on old logging roads as far as we could go from home. Then we packed our outfit into the timber on our backs. The sun was three hours high when we had pitched the lodge and gathered dry alders for firewood. I left Charley to cut fir boughs for our beds and straighten up camp and struck out for meat. Luckily, I killed a deer before sundown not more than two miles from camp. I hurried preparation of the deer for packing on my back and struck out for the lodge. But darkness had come before I got there. "Meat," I sang out as I approached.

Charley, the best of camp partners, had a fire burning and was baking bannocks. I dropped my pack and stepped into the lodge. A pair of pliers, reflecting the firelight, caught my attention. Why were they there? They belonged in the car. I picked them up and saw blood on them. "Did I drop these out of my pocket?" I asked, wiping the pliers on the sleeve of my buckskin shirt.

[3] That is, they dissolved partnership.

"Nope, I went down to the car an' got 'em," he replied, busy with his bannocks.

"You must have needed them badly," I said, wondering about the blood on them.

"Did, by God," he muttered, grimly. "Had a tooth that was achin'. Thought it was a damn sight looser than it was an' I wasn't goin' to let it spoil this trip for me. So I went down an' got the pliers, stuck 'em into some boilin' water, an' then pulled the tooth."

"Why, you brave old devil," I marveled.

"Brave, hell," he snapped. "I got a good hold on that tooth an' give her hell right quick. I twisted an' turned her like them dentists do; but I couldn't fetch her. She was bolted in. I had to give her up, feelin' damn sorry I'd started the job."

He stacked his bannocks, chuckling now. "When I tried to shut my mouth I couldn't do it. She wouldn't go shut." He laughed. "That damned tooth I'd pulled on was more'n an inch longer'n any of the others, so I plumb had to go through with the job or go hungry. When I got her out I was blubbering like a hurt kid. Here she is."

The tooth had roots like those of a fir stump. Charley was full of pure grit.

*Frank Linderman had told himself for years
that when he had money enough to secure the safety of
his family he would build a house on Flathead Lake and
devote himself to writing about Indians of an older day
and the early West. In 1917 his dream came to fruition.
The log house on Goose Bay was large and attractive. It
sat well up from the shore line among evergreen and
deciduous trees and brush, with hills sloping up to the
south and west. The curve of the bay ended to the south
in a rocky outthrust and to the north in a low-lying point
of land. To this beautiful spot and this lovely home with
its welcoming family, Charley Russell loved to come.*[1]

[1] Verne Linderman, the second daughter, wrote for *The Christian Science Monitor* in 1942 an article entitled "The Big Lonesome": "So the cabin was built, of larch logs. . . . It occupied the center of a square bay on Flathead Lake. The wooded slopes came down like sheltering arms from the hills behind the house. There was not a neighbor on either side; only virgin timber back of us, and before us, rimmed on the far shore by blue mountains, ten or twelve miles away."

FOUR · AT GOOSE BAY,
FLATHEAD LAKE

CHARLEY was with us when, in November, 1917, we moved into our log house at Goose Bay, joyfully helping us unpack our household goods, his boots clumping from room to room on the uncovered floors, his witticisms quickening merriment in us all. "Busy as a gal eatin' soup with her hatpin," he laughed as I passed him in the hall, his arms full of bedding.[2]

The house was unfinished. No daubing had been done, and the wind blew through the chinking between the logs. The furnace had not been installed. Except for the fire in the kitchen range that crackled assuringly and the one in the big fireplace in the living room there was no heat. Boxes and barrels, excelsior and wads of paper littered the floors. Hudson's Bay blankets tacked to studding gave the bedrooms a suggestion of privacy. Each of us knew his room by the color of the enclosing blanket.

Our forest surroundings and the great stretch of lake filled us with joy. Our meals were marvels of merriment, owing in part to Charley's apt comments on improvised dishes. During our

[2] Verne Linderman in the same article: "Almost every year, when *Napi* was painting the leaves of the moose maples, Charley and our father, Frank Linderman, who had received his name of Sign-Talker from the Indians, had liked to go hunting. Even now, when they no longer approved of hunting wild game for sport, they still got together. For Charley to live in, we pitched our Thunder Lodge—painted long ago for Sign-Talker by the Blackfeet women, Mrs. Buffalo-Body and Mrs. Running-Rabbit—on the northern point of the bay. Mornings, Charley would hobble over the trail strewn with frost-wet, yellow larch needles, in his high-heeled boots, the ends of his *voyageur* sash swinging, his breath white in the chill air. 'How! How! Hi-ee! How's the Swiss Family Robinson today?' he would call."

43

first dinner a coyote, attracted by the candlelight from our un-curtained windows, howled in the brush near the house, stop-ping Charley's cup near his lips. "Wow!" he marveled, tiptoeing to the window and shading his eyes. "Makes me homesick for the old days." His voice was solemn. "This is sure a dandy place, Frank. I saw a whole lot of fresh deer tracks near the porch this afternoon."

More than breezes came through the chinking—deer mice and mountain rats came too, and they were pests that got into everything. Charley complained when a rat had packed away his socks, "I don't mind 'em being chummy with me in daylight but I don't like 'em to sleep with me." The mice troubled us until the house was finished. But we got rid of the mountain rats. Night or day the appearance of one of them called us all to battle. In their devilish mischief, mostly at night, they made as much noise as dogs and wantonly damaged things until daylight, and then they often bedded down upon the scene of their reveling to wait for darkness to come again.

One afternoon while Charley was taking his nap, his snoring terrible to hear, the girls discovered a mountain rat behind a large box in the living room; they called to me and all of us went into action without a thought of our sleeping guest. "Here he is, Daddy. No, there he goes. He's behind that barrel now. There, there, on the log. See him?" Bang! My rifle ended the excited rumpus just as the scarlet-blanket partition of our guest room lifted and Charley, his straw-colored hair tousled and his shirt unbuttoned at the neck, appeared. "What the hell's goin' on here, gals? Camp attacked by Injins?" he called, his voice brisk,

44

his swift hands winding his red sash round his waist. "Got him!" he said, as with the toe of his boot he moved the rat. " 'Course, we don't know everything," he went on, serious now, "but if God made nothin' in vain I wish somebody would show me some good in a mountain rat. I sure can't see it if it's there an' I been lookin' for it ever since I was a kid."

We had a pet that had chosen our company which for two years visited us nightly at Goose Bay, a flying squirrel we named Tommy. I had lived most of my life in the open country, and yet I have never known a flying squirrel, except Tommy, to take up with men. I nearly shot him, mistaking him for a rat, on his first visit. Only a glimpse of his black, expressionless eyes in the candlelight had saved his life. Happy that I had recognized him in time, I left him a saucer of milk and bread. Thereafter for two years at about a quarter of nine each evening Tommy came for his bread and milk, always making enough noise to let us know that he had arrived.

Tommy was a great joy for Charley: "Lemme feed him this time," he would say, holding the saucer in the candlelight. The squirrel ate out of the saucer while we held it and even took bits of cake from our fingers. When Charley came to Goose Bay a year later, his first question was, "How's Tommy?" And when he saw Tommy he said, "God, ain't his tail pretty?"

One morning when I opened the shed door I saw Tommy's beautiful tail lying in the trail to the woodpile. A blood-hunting cat, gone wild in the forest, had eaten him. We sent Tommy's tail to Charley.

In 1919, because the old road along the shore of the lake was rough the whole way from Goose Bay to Somers, about twelve miles, I built a sailboat, the *Vigilante*. She was twenty-two feet over-all, with a beam of eight feet, and she sailed well. We made many trips in her to Somers for supplies and several times to fetch Charley from the railroad to Goose Bay. One hot afternoon when the two of us arrived in the *Vigilante* the girls met us at the door: "Come and see what this animal is that's on Babe's bed!" They were excited. A half-grown weasel squealed angrily at us from the center of the white spread. "Kinda likes it there, don't he?" Charley laughed. "Let's catch the cuss."

We put him in a wooden box covered with a window screen. The savage beast leaped at us whenever we approached the box. "Ain't he narvy?" Charley marveled. "The dirty little murderer! By God, I bet if them fellers growed as big as house cats they'd run us all off the earth."

At dinner, he asked, his eyes scanning each of us in turn, "Well, what are we going to do with the little pet?" Nobody answered the query. "Goin' to turn him loose or kill him?"

"Ought to be killed," I said.

"Yep. But anyway, let's feed him some of this ice cream first." Charley replenished his dish and went outside, followed by Mrs. Linderman and the girls.

We had installed an electric lighting plant, and no longer had to depend upon candles. Charley carried the box beneath a light and managed to get his dish of ice cream into it, spilling a little. The weasel, after licking up what was spilled, cleaned the dish.

But it made him sick at his stomach. The audience except Charley and me faded away.

"Wow! Shall we kill him?" Charley asked, carrying the box out of the basement and setting it on the grass gingerly. "He's sick as hell," he said, looking at the beast.

"Ought to be killed," I asserted again.

"Yeah, but the poor little devil's awful sick." After a moment he added, "But he'll die anyway. Mebby we ought to let him go, hey?" Charley's hand was on the screen ready to take it off, his eyes inquiring of me.

"All right," I agreed.

Like a flash our patient was gone—to grow up and kill the gentler kind in the forests.

"I reckon we ought to 'uv killed him," Charley muttered, his eyes on the dark timber. "But God made 'em. An' he made snakes, an' mountain rats, an' a lot of things we don't savvy."

It was a great privilege to know Charley intimately and to be with him as Christmas drew near. He was happy as a child in his secret work upon the gifts—small pictures, models of animals, dolls, and gnomes so grotesque in form and posture that that they were received only with happy laughter. As the great day approached, he tiptoed about his "shack" and grew more and more mysterious. The slight bow in his legs was emphasized by his short, quick steps in his high-heeled riding boots. The fringed end of his red sash, which he was never without, dangled at his side. He was the very image of a small boy bent upon mischief.

47

He loved Christmas. He loved to make gifts for his friends, especially out of strange materials.[3] Anything at hand, out-of-doors things preferred, that could be turned to surprising use challenged him. Here at Goose Bay, where he liked so much to be, he and our daughter Verne spent many happy hours painting little wooden girls and dressing their figures with leaves colored beautifully by the sharp November night. They raced around the moose maples, the birches, and the cottonwoods laughing gleefully, gathering doll clothes from their branches—"shopping at Birch and Company" they called it. Their following contests to dress their dolls becomingly attracted us all. We watched them eagerly as they huddled about the dining table strewn with autumn leaves, tubes of paint and glue, forgetting bedtime, forgetting even to feed the fire.

"Oh, wow!" Charley would chuckle, holding up a leaf-attired doll for us to admire. "Wow! She looks tough, like she's been eatin' hoss shoes. Lemme see yours, Verne."

This would go on and on. Some of the dolls were beautiful indeed; but unfortunately, they never lasted beyond a day or two. Their daintily colored clothes withered on bookcases and tables until at last the fireplace got them all.

"I can't paint a white woman," Charley told me one night after

[3] "At Christmastime he would make little religious figures, carefully colored, and similar objects depicted on paper in water color for his friends, both young and old." (McCracken, *op. cit.*, 204.) "Most of Charlie's poetry was written around Christmas holidays. During his life he took a childish delight in preparing for this occasion. He made models of reindeer and Santa Claus for the festive table. The joys of his boyhood homelife seemed to return a thousand fold at this time." (Adams and Britzman, *op. cit.*, 273).

48

a doll-making spree. "Every time I paint a white woman she looks tough as nails. If I paint her over again she looks tougher, like a hooker."

He did indeed seldom paint white women. I have one that he painted. Her costume is exquisite, perfect in every detail; she herself answers Charley's description of his white women: she is unmistakably of the demimonde.

The last time Charley was here Mrs. Linderman laughingly reminded him of an incident which had occurred while we were settling into the household. The fireplace was then without a mantel; two gaping caverns nearly six feet deep and more than four feet wide led down into blackness on each side. The supports for the mantel were handy places for things that suddenly got in the way.

Charley and I had pitched an Indian lodge on the north point of the bay,[4] visiting there evenings and sleeping there nights. Often we cooked our supper in the lodge to save troubling the busy women in the house. Mrs. Linderman, however, frequently supplied us with bread and tidbits, which we carried to our camp. Late one afternoon she placed a pan of hot rolls upon the mantel supports beside a box of candles and advised us to take them to the lodge before they got cold. We were anxious to do so not only because we were ready to go but because the day was cold.

"See you in the mornin'," Charley said, reaching for the pan of rolls. His boots slipped on the hearth of the fireplace. Down went the pan and the box of candles into the deep hole. The

[4] Now a camping ground, but still a part of the Linderman estate.

blank and startled look on Charley's face sent us all into spasms of laughter.

"Come on, Russ, let's go," I said when I could speak.

But no, Charley was determined to recover the rolls and candles. He began to fish for them immediately, changing his implements a dozen times before midnight. His dogged efforts amused and distracted us all. He finally got the empty pan. Near noon the next day he had fished up a few rolls, that nobody wanted, but he could not land a single candle. The hole has been sealed for twenty years, and the candles and the rolls may be still in it.

When on August 17, 1919, a forest fire swept Goose Bay clean except for the house, nobody felt the loss more than Charley. He had been with us a few days before, but fires at Lake McDonald, where his own cabin was, had called him there. He and I had been camped on the point in a lodge painted with thirty-six figures by Indian friends. The paintings delighted Charley, as usual. One of the pictures was of an old warrior chasing a horse, a coiled rope in his hand, his hair flying. This picture had so interested Charley that he had sketched it as a masterpiece of Indian art. The fire burned the lodge and all in it, even the anchor line of the *Vigilante* in the bay, setting her adrift in the blinding smoke. Later, standing on the site of the painted lodge, his boots in its ashes, Charley turned his eyes to the sailboat. "You got her again," he said, "but you'll never get another painted lodge like that one was. An' now that poor old Injin will never catch the hoss."

Eighteen years have passed since then. The marks of the devastating fire are nearly obliterated; yet long before the young trees are grown to the size of those destroyed I shall be looking for Charley's campfire in the Shadow Hills.

*Charley Russell lived for six months in 1888
with the Bloods, a branch of the Blackfeet Indians living
in Alberta, Canada, and seriously considered, at their urging and something of his own inclination, settling among
them.[1] He became a member of the tribe and was known
as Ah-wah-cous (Horns That Fork, or Antelope). His
Pikuni name was Running Antelope. Linderman had
known several tribes, at first the Flatheads or Salishes,
then the Blackfeet, then the Crees and Chippewas, and
later the Crows. He was adopted into three tribes: the
Blackfeet, who gave him the name of Mex-shim-yo-peek-
kinny (Iron Tooth); the Crees, who called him Co-skee-
see-co-cot (The Man Who Looks Through Glass); and
the Crows, among whom he was Mah-paht-sa-mot-tsas
(Sign-Talker).*

[1] Russell considered being a squaw man and ". . . there is evidence that his
contemplation of the matter was a fairly serious one." (McCracken, *op. cit.,*
113.) "Sleeping Thunder, a chief of the Bloods urged him [Russell] to forsake
the path of the white man and to marry one of the Indian women." (Adams
and Britzman, *op. cit.,* 95.) Nancy Russell, in *Good Medicine*, wrote that the
Indians urged him to marry into their tribe. When among the Bloods in
Canada for about six months, "one of his beautiful subjects . . . was a lovely
Indian maiden, Kee-oh-mee, who wore the snow-white elkskin garments of
a chief's daughter. . . . She carried herself with simple dignity and a charm
that would not have been lost in any sophisticated gathering. She was vivacious
and fun loving, and, had Charlie looked on her with romantic inclinations, he
would have found himself with a field of competitors for her hand." See Shelton, *op. cit.,* 100, 103–105; see also McCracken, *op. cit.,* 110.

IN 1912 the Pikunis sent me an invitation to be present at a tribal powwow. Word reached me that they had pitched an old buffalo skin lodge in the center of their temporary village for my use. On the way there I stopped at Great Falls and got Charley to go with me to Fort Browning. We expected to reach there by dark, but the train was very late and landed us there some time after ten o'clock. Our old friends, nevertheless, were waiting for us and escorted us to the lodge they had prepared for me. There they serenaded us for an hour or more before going to their own fires. A lone half-blood was left, who stuck to us like a tick, probably thinking that we had liquor in our outfit which we would share with him. We wanted to go to bed but could not rid ourselves of the fellow without asking him outright to leave, and this we did not like to do.

A misty rain began to fall and the night grew extremely dark. The old skin lodge became sodden; our guest became a greater bore by the minute; Charley's exaggerated yawning gave him no hint that he took. Suddenly a squall of wind brought us the sound of drums, faint and faraway.

"Did you hear that?" Charley asked, leaning forward in the firelight. But a quick shower of heavy rain suddenly shut out the sound.

I listened intently. "Sounded like a Sun Dance."

"Yeah, dat's de Sun Dance. Dem Cree she's dance por two day now," the half-blood told us disinterestedly.

"Wow! Wish I could see 'em dancin' in the firelight. How far away are they?" Charley asked, going to the lodge door.

" 'Bout a mile, mebby two. But you can't get in dere. Dey won't let nobody but de Cree in dat Sun dance. She's no damn good, dem damn Cree." Our friend was emphatic.

Soon the shower had passed and a fine, misty rain took its place. Now, outside of the lodge, we could hear the drums plainly. They were beyond the wide circle of Blackfeet lodges. The wind brought us the voices of singers along with the drums.

"I never saw a Sun Dance in firelight," Charley said wistfully, his face toward the distant sounds.

"You say it's the Crees who are dancing?" I asked the half-blood.

"Yeah, dem damn Cree. Little Bear, she's de chief. She's mean wan, dat man."

"Come on, Russ," I said, "they can't do more than kick us out." I headed for the sounds, Charley at my heels.

No darkness could ever be blacker. The great circle of Blackfeet lodges, marked by firelight here and there, must have been more than a mile across. We had no slickers; the rain was soaking our clothing; but we pushed north toward the drums.[2] As we passed among lodges on the rim of the village two dogs rushed us furiously. One of them tore my pants. "Don't run, Russ," I warned. We backed away slowly, and the dogs left us.

"By God, we sure shook our little half-blood friend, anyway." Charley was pleased, now free of the Indian and the dogs. "Hope we can get in," he said, his voice expressing his wish.

The sun lodge was now in sight, and little lances of firelight

[2] The lodge of the two men was in the Pikuni circle of lodges; they walked across this circle toward the Cree celebration of the Sun Dance.

were darting through its sagebrush-covered sides. A voice deep and stern, nearly angry in tone, was haranguing the dancers. The whistles were quiet, the drums silent when we reached the entrance. Charley hesitated, his hand on my arm, "By God, I don't know about this butting in," he said.

But I recognized the voice. "Come on." I took his arm and we stepped into the sun lodge. Instantly the harangue stopped. The speaker turned, anger flashing in his dark eyes. Naked except for a breechcloth, he sprang toward us; then he stopped and seized my hand, "Ho Ho, Hi-eeeeeeee," he shouted, his painted arm slipping about my shoulders. He led us to the center pole and welcomed us feelingly. Reaching up, he took from the pole an old otter skin bedecked with eagle feathers, hawk bells, and medicine and handed it to me. "This belonged to my grand-father, my father, and me, all chiefs of the Crees. I give it to you now. Hold it fast. It is big medicine."[3] Turning to the drummer he cried, "Ho!" and the dance was on again—in the firelight.

No host can be more gracious than an old Indian. The speaker, Chief Little Bear, found good seats for us on the grass and him-self sat beside us. The shrill, eagle-wing whistles, the drumming, the singers, the painted faces, the weird headdresses fascinated Charley. "Oh, no, we can't get in here, I guess!" he chuckled happily, in deep satisfaction, and got out his sketchbook.

"No, no," I warned him, "Don't make any sketches here. They'd object. Just soak up what you see and sketch it in camp."

Hours passed. Finally, shaking Little Bear's hand and in-viting him to our lodge when the Sun Dance was finished, we

[3] It is still in the Linderman collection of Indian objects.

left. It was daylight. Charley spoke not a word all the way to our lodge. People were already stirring in the Blackfeet village, the men going out after horses and the women bringing kettles of water. Smoke was curling from hundreds of tipis.

"I wouldn't have missed seeing that for a thousand dollars," Charley said. "The dancin' in that firelight was great." He sat down with his sketchbook.

"By God," he thought back as he sketched, "if you ever turn desperado you'll be plumb safe if you can get to your Crees."

If he ever painted a picture of the Sun Dance in firelight, I never saw it.

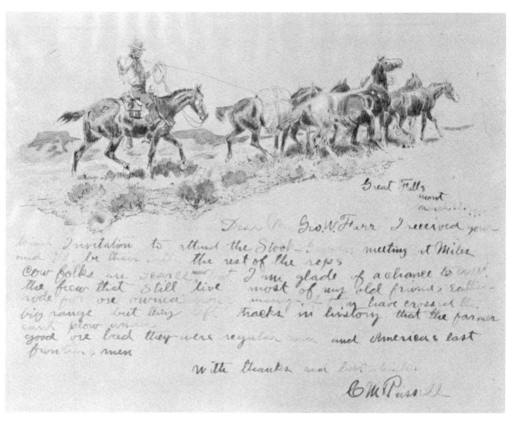

Atop this letter Russell drew a self-portrait, showing himself as a horse-wrangler.

Charley with Jake Hoover in the Belt Mountains.

"Roundup"

Courtesy of F. G. Renner

"Quick Shooting Saves Our Lives"

This trip has been noticed in biographies of Russell but never intimately or so fully. Since the Lewis and Clark expedition the Missouri has, of course, been often explored and has attracted amateur scientists and tourists. The most visited stretches, however, have been the Great Falls region and the Gates of the Mountains. Fort Clagett, mentioned here, was located at the mouth of the Judith River; the trip was therefore from Fort Benton down the river to Fort Clagett. The location was difficult to get at other than by river, so that the fort did not last long.

Austin Russell asserts that this trip "had a lasting effect on Charlie's art . . . now he began to paint those ruddy sunsets with Indian figures, not white men," which to Austin Russell seemed to have "more magic than all his previous pictures."

CHARLEY and I had often talked of seeing the badlands along the Missouri River, particularly those about old Fort Clagett. We wanted to see them by boat so that we could stop anywhere, tie up, and explore. One autumn we ordered the craft to be built at Fort Benton. When it was ready we outfitted there. Four were in the party this time: my father, then an elderly man, Dr. Nash, Charley, and myself. I don't recall the year when we set out down the Missouri, but the month was September.[1]

On the boat's stern, to speed us along when the current lagged, was an outboard motor, an engine which was new at that time and often temperamental. Ours was possessed of all faults and no virtues. Poor Dr. Nash, our engineer, softly swearing, cranked and tinkered for days. Finally, we decided to stow the smelly thing under the deck. Besides wearing Doc down, it had flavored our food and made our blankets reek with the odor of gasoline.

"Why not pitch it overboard?" Charley asked.

"Gosh, we can't; it belongs to Ralph DeCamp," said Doc.

"A man's got to be an electrician, an engineer, a plumber, an' a master mechanic to get anything out of that rig but a stink. An' by God, he'd ought to be a preacher, too, or he'd sure go straight to hell when he died." Charley was amused in spite

[1] Austin Russell, *op. cit.*, 219: "When it came to stowing the cargo on the boat they discovered that either it was more bulky than they had figured or the scow was less roomy; and about every third item seemed to be soap. 'I didn't know this was a business trip,' said Charlie, 'Doc must be starting a laundry.' 'Hell!' said Frank, at his most impatient, 'that's too much soap!' and threw it overboard . . . they went the rest of the way without washing."

of annoyance. We were all disgusted. We shoved the motor under the deck.

Drifting along in the fine weather, we kept the boat in the current with occasional paddling. The badlands on both sides of the river were wonderful and grotesque. We stopped often to wander among their tables, chairs, stools, harps, battleships, and holes. The grotesque and the beautiful were side by side as though to teach appreciation by contrasts.

One afternoon, separated by our individual interests in the fantastic figures and about a half-mile from the river, I happened to look his way and saw Charley stumble and fall. I ran to him. "Hurt yourself?" I asked anxiously.

"Nope," he said, scrambling to his feet on the caved rim of a deep hole. "It would be a dirty trick to play on the badlands; but here's a damned good place to cache our stinker for keeps." He dropped a stone into the hole and listened for it to hit bottom. "I'd like to pitch it in myself and hear it go 'plunk.' " The shape of the hole had interested him; he called it a giant's wineglass. He had almost fallen into it, and limped from his scrambling for several days afterward.

Our first bad luck came to us when we shoved off after this visit to the shore. The current, which here was swifter than it had been, swept the boat against a hidden rock, and the impact tore a board from her transom. By the time we had reached shallow water and leaped overboard the boat was filled with water and everything in it, of course, was thoroughly soaked.

We unloaded our outfit and spread blankets and grub out in the hot sun to dry and got the boat to shore and turned her bottom-side up. We examined her and found that she had been hurriedly built with nails and that presented difficulties, for the only tool we had was an ax. We had only the nails we could pound out of the board and straighten. We thought they would do. The calking was gone from two seams about four feet long. We of course had no oakum. After propping the boat on its side and building a great fire to help the sun dry the boat, we spread out in search of pitch. But, as luck would have it, only cottonwood trees grew at this spot. We shredded our handkerchiefs and the pockets cut from our coats and, making a calking tool out of serviceberry wood, pounded the rags into the seams. This, we thought, gave us calking enough.

By the time we had eaten supper the sun and the fire had dried the boat's bottom so much that we could work on it in the morning. By sundown most of our blankets were dry; but Charley's pillow, which had been left in the shade of a bush, was as wet as ever. "I'll fix her," he said, stripping off the slip and hanging the pillow near the big fire. I saw that dark, shoddy cotton stuck out of a rip in the casing and thought it would make much better calking than any we had used. I took a handful from the steaming pillow and pounded it into a seam. I breathed a bit of satisfaction that the twinkling stars had brought us that good luck.

But the stars did not twinkle for us long; before midnight clouds had covered them and a chill wind blew down the river. While our partners slept Charley and I kept the fire going so that the boat would dry more. "Equinoctial comin'?" he asked, turning up the collar of his coat. "Hope we can find a good camp before she hits us." He was warming a piece of modeling wax before the fire, his fingers working it idly.

"What's in the stuff? What's it made of?" I asked, for the idea of using it for pitch on our boat had occurred to me.

"Nothing but beeswax an' a little tallow," he answered, handing me the wax.

"Got any more?"

"Some in my war bag." He snatched his scorching pillow from beside the fire. "She's dry," he told me gleefully and feeling the hot casing flung the pillow onto some blankets inside the tent.

Early in the morning we applied the beeswax to the seams and by nine o'clock pushed off on our way down the river. "Bet a good hoss we're the first fellers that ever mended a ship with a pillow and modeling wax," he chuckled, holding tight to the rim of his hat.

A little later rain began falling. "Toss me that slicker, Doc," Charley called. "Let's us all keep lookin' for some fresh meat an' a good place to camp. We're sure goin' to need 'em both."

"There, Dad, there!" He pointed to two ducks putting out from shore.

My father's shot killed them both. They were a strange pair, one a ruddy and the other a mud hen.

Charley was closely examining the feet of the mud hen. "Is this kind good to eat? Never saw a duck that had feet like this thing."

I told him it was but he thought he was being hoaxed. "Dad," he said, "see if you can kill a hoot owl so's we can make a stew. A fat hoot owl ought to flavor this thing." He began plucking

61

the mud hen, nevertheless, the high wind strewing feathers in all directions.

The storm increased. Squalls of icy wind made navigation so difficult that we frequently got stuck on bars. We had to get out into the cold water in order to lighten the boat and float her off. At two o'clock in the afternoon we camped at a miserable spot and hurriedly put up our tent.

Stiff with cold, we began a search for dry wood. The gumbo was so sticky that we could scarcely walk. The rain turned to sleet. We found some heavy oak beams and planking from a long-wrecked steamboat half buried in the river's bank. Some of the timbers were twenty feet long and heavy as lead. But we dragged them to camp and piled them as backlogs for the fire. When they finally burned their flames were multicolored, greens and reds and purples and their ashes brick red. The flames skipped along the old steamboat's timbers like footlights on a stage.

Charley, watching them, said, "A ghost dance of the old river days."

We all wondered what steamboat we were burning. "If a man painted them little flames just like they are they'd run him out of town. What do you reckon makes 'em so pretty? Salt?" he wondered. I told him that when I was a boy I had seen sailors use strong brine to preserve the timbers of their vessels; they forced it into auger holes and then plugged the holes. "Mebby," he admitted. "Time an' salt an' gumbo can do a hell of a lot of things." Like the rest of us, he was scraping the heavy loads of mud off his boots. "By God, if a sage hen would happen to light anywhere around this camp we could walk right out an' pick 'er up. It's a cinch she couldn't walk an' the gumbo on her feet would weight 'er down so's she couldn't fly."

The stew, with dumplings, spuds, and coffee, brightened us. The mud hen, however, was indistinguishable from the duck. But our hastily put up tent was sagging with wet snow and hung not far above our noses when we turned in. Charley and Doc, as usual, were sleeping together.

A coyote yelped in the storm not far from our fire. "There's one of your old friends, Russ," Doc said.

"Yeah, I heard 'im. He wants to borrow my slicker." He sat up, his nose sniffling. "Say, Doc, is your breechcloth afire? Somethin's burnin' in here."

"Shut your little eyes and go to sleep. Nothing could burn in here—nor out there," Doc declared after a look at our struggling fire. "I don't smell anything." They both settled down and were snoring within minutes.

Near midnight Father and I were roused by Charley shouting, "What the hell's goin' on here?" He was sitting up in bed and staring at Doc, who was trying to shield the blaze of a match against the wind in his cupped hands.

"Something *is* afire in this tent," Doc said, trying to strike another match. His efforts to find a dry place sent Charley into a fit of chuckling.

"What the hell you laughing at?" Doc snapped, as at last a match flame flared.

"Laughin' at a man that wants a light to find fire in the dark," Charley snorted.

We were now all laughing. Doc and Charley were tumbling their blankets to find the fire. Snow was blowing into the uncovered front of our tent, whitening the foot of our beds. The raw wind was bellying the heavy canvas. We all four settled down once more; but not for long.

"Hey, Russ, wake up, man, wake up!" Doc was shaking Charley and of course waking Father and me.

Doc lighted a candle. "It's your pillow, Russ," he laughed. A thin film of smoke was issuing from the shoddy beneath Charley's head. "Don't you see, man?"

"I'll fix her good an' plenty," Charley said sleepily. He poured three tin cups of water into the hole in the pillow. Doc offered him the end of his pillow. "Nope, I can use the other end of mine," he declared.

The shoddy had caught fire while we had been drying the boat the day before and had been afire ever since. Rolled tightly in the blankets, the fire had had no air and had smoldered until now. Twice more before morning Charley poured water into the pillow's hole, and still the fire persisted. Two days later, the fire unquenched, Charley threw the pillow into the Missouri. "By God, if our grandads had had that thing, they could've had fire all their lives without having to borrow coals from their neighbors." We watched the pillow float downstream.

The morning was disgusting. Snow and slippery gumbo were everywhere, wind and water in everything, and not a stick of dry wood anywhere. But we had to have a fire. The half-buried pile of old steamboat timbers offered our best prospect for wood. Sliding and slipping and even falling down, we eventually got another pile of wood into camp. Nobody cared a rap about the color of the flames this time.

Three more days we huddled in this miserable place—each day, each hour worse than the one before. The tent and all were enough to give anyone the willies. Everybody's hair was pulling; nobody was good-natured. Doc inadvertently set Charley off into a tirade against Bob Ingersoll by making a short quotation from him.

Charley ended up saying, "That dirty infidel never said a word or did a thing that was worth remembering for ten seconds." He went away muttering to himself.

The next morning as I started the fire I shouted, "Well, boys, the sun's going to shine. We'll have breakfast, bail out the boat, and move. Yippee!" Near noon we made camp in a delightful little park beside the river. The bright sun was wiping away the snow, leaving the land refreshed and beautiful. The gumbo, however, was heavy and slippery. I followed deer signs along the river in search of fresh meat, lifting my feet, heavy with a weight of gumbo, wearily. Before dark I had a buck and dragged him into camp. "What's that you got?" inquired Doc. It looked like a great mound of mud. "Why bring any more mud into camp?"

Charley, delighting in the prospect of fresh meat, helped me skin and cut up the deer. My father, who was always anxious to do his share of camp work, was annoyed by our refusal to let him help.

"That old man's good leather, good's any one of us right now. An' he's a damn good pardner. You know," Charley went on,

65

"somebody has said that if he'd a'had God's job of makin' things he'd a'made men grow young instead of old and he'd a'made good health catchin' instead of sickness."

"Are you in on all that, Russ?" I asked as innocently as I could, for I wanted to get him hooked.

"I sure am. Why if . . ."

"Hold on," I stopped him, "do you know who said that, Russ?"

"No, who?"

"Bob Ingersoll," I said. A mere glance at Charley's eyes made me sorry I had hooked him. I decided against further comment.

The weather turned warm, so warm that we had to jerk our venison to save it. Festoons of drying meat, two joints of stovepipe we never used, and two equally useless wagon bows gave us the appearance of a dry-land farmer moving out of the country. And when at last I rigged a sail for the boat, she and our camp defied description.

Charley had with him the journals of Lewis and Clark. Sometimes he read paragraphs aloud, particularly when they were about our surroundings. His reading was like that of a small boy. He frequently spelled out words for our pronunciation. "Them old boys could go *up* this river with a load an' we can't even go *down* the damned thing without getting stuck forty times a day," he said as he stepped into the water to get the boat off a bar.

In this illustrated letter to "Friend Frank," Charley deplores the exploitation of nature by the white man.

Courtesy of Dr. Van Kirke Nelson

Friend Frank   Sept 14
          I received your kind invitation   1912
an would shure like to go. all the more since I eat an
smoked with you over a lodge fire
I looked you over pritty thorough Frank an from the out
side you dont show much Injun but by the way
you look to
                                        that skin lodge
y think   if you will slide
back   on your family
tree   youl find
Lindermans   that wore skins
an smelt   of willow bark
                                        any thing in
If thares   when you
re incarnation   here before
wer   nane was
your   Lean Man
                                        or Long Man

Its a   sinch it wasent Linderman
them days   you wore a clout an smoked
with the sun   He was your God an you asked no better
death seldom caught your kind in bed an when he came
it onely ment a better country with more buffalo
you wer not selfish your religon said all things
lived again
you were a heathen but your prayers were longer
an more frequent than your Christian brothers

A colorful letter to Linderman, written in 1912.

In this life your words were feew
buffalo that romed your country in millions
gave meat clothes and a good house
baring a feew roots an berries you were
as carriverious as your brother the wolf
who followed the heards like your self
from birds shells an the porcupine your women decked
your body in clothes
sometimes you turned over an enemy an gathered
hair to trim your leggions this you raised
with out irrigation often this went the
other way when this happened
your trimmer found a neat brade down your
back making a handy
hand holt for the Saviner
gatherer
You are not quite as raw now Frank as you
were when you were ~~when~~ on earth before
but still show strong croppings of the
savig
an as I am your kind my self. Bill and
I will meet you at Somers oct first
With regards to you and yours
your friend CM Russell

Courtesy of Norma Linderman Waller

*"An Enemy That Warns," a bronze by Charles M. Russell.
Two foes of the cattlemen of Russell's era: the wolf and the
rattlesnake.*

Both Russell and Linderman loved country,
Russell the more open country east of the Rockies and
Linderman the more mountainous country west of them.
Both men loved simple, primitive life in the open. Neither
cared for the city or life in it. Both loathed the pretences
of people who felt that they had to keep up with one another. Both were frank, open in thought and talk. Both
were modest, and yet had something of the showman in
them, partly in defense of the West, especially when
among city people. Both had a sort of we-are-different
spirit, with perhaps a hidden feeling that their way of
life—the early life of the West—was much better. Thinking that, both would doubtless add, "Well, anyway, I like
it better."

It was Mrs. Russell and the need for exhibiting and sell-
ing Charley's pictures and sculptures that took him to New

York City annually for several years. It was the need for placing his writings with publishers that took Linderman there at one time for seven months.

In society both men preserved Western individuality, Russell wearing his voyageur *sash, even with a dress suit, and his high-heeled cowboy boots, and Linderman wearing his broad-brimmed Western hat and some of the time his sash.*

Both men would have subscribed to the later thought of Eric Sevareid, published in the Saturday Review *of October 20, 1962: "You think empty space diminishes the individual, makes him feel lost and little? Any individual who feels that way in the mountains or on the prairies has felt lost and little all his life. It's crowds and close quarters that make most of us feel lost and little."*

CHARLEY RUSSELL'S trips to New York City to find a market for his paintings and sculptures were replete with experiences he never forgot. I recount only one of those he spoke of to me:

"WE didn't have any money when me and Mame first landed in the big town. An' Frank, it's the lonesomest camp on earth. By God, I'd be tickled to death to have met a rattlesnake I'd seen before. Our room, way up off the ground, had only one window an' it opened on a dirty brick wall that wasn't more'n two feet away. Air? Wow! It smelled like the dump pile behind old Frank Lampman's chuck wagon. An' we had to keep our light burnin' all day.

"I used to look down to the bottom of that narrow, black hole wonderin' if they ever cleaned it out or if they could get in there *to* clean it out. There was a cat that ranged there. She was the color of the hole an' no thicker'n my hand an' so weak she staggered huntin' somethin' to eat. She was always there an' always huntin'. I used to put pieces of meat in my pocket when we ate at restaurants an' drop 'em down to the cat. God, how she'd nail 'em! You'd think they'd make her savvy there was better range some place else an' that she'd get out of there. But no sir, she was a New Yorker. By God, she'd rather stay in that dirty hole an' starve than get out where she could get clean air and live decently. An' there's a hell of a lot of people like that cat. They stay in New York an' damn near starve because they like the excitement of the crowd—that's what they call havin'

69

their toes trampled on forty times a day. She's not for me an' she ain't for you, Frank.[1]

"Well, finally Mame opened up an exhibit some place, I don't remember where, but the lightin' was rotten. Of course, I had to show up there once in a while. One day a painter who was lookin' at my pictures asked me to his place for a feed an' I said I'd go. I guess he didn't have the price of our carfare an' it was a cinch I didn't, so we walked an' walked an' walked till we came to a bridge that everybody in New York wanted to cross just at that time. God! We just inched along afeelin' folks breathin' down our necks. We was just like a herd of cattle crowdin' through a brandin' chute. I couldn't see my feet; didn't know whether I had boots on or moccasins 'cept when they got stepped on. But everybody was good-natured an' nobody ornery. All of a sudden we got jammed, stopped still. A feller sings out, 'This is what I call livin', Harold,' 'By God,' I says so's he'd hear, an' knowin' he couldn't get at me even if he wanted to, 'You'd oughta been a maggot, pardner.' "

England

CHARLEY and Mame visited England in 1914. Charley was captivated by the beauty of the countryside and by the love Englishmen had for tradition. "They ain't ashamed of old ways over

[1] One remembers the often-quoted remark of Russell, found again in Shelton, *op. cit.,* 155: "New York is all right, but not for me. It's too big and there are too many tall tepees. I'd rather live in a place where I know somebody, and where everybody is somebody. Here everybody is somebody but there you've got to be a millionaire to be *any* body."

there," he told me on his return. "They're proud of 'em. Even
to this day they do things just because Englishmen did 'em
hundreds of years ago. An' do you know, that keeps 'em on the
trail that made their country great. An' say, they ain't in such
a hell of a hurry as we are, neither."

I shall never forget his account of a dinner given in his honor
by Lord ———.[2] "A feller that looked like he mighta played
marbles with old Oliver Cromwell when they was kids let us in
the front door. He was in knee pants an' had big silver buckles
on his shoes an' a fluffy collar. He takes my hat an' leads us to
another feller who'd somehow got out of another old picture
book, an' this feller announced us at the door of a big room that
had a floor that looked like a roller skatin' rink, "Mistah and
Missus Chahles Russell,' he calls out, turnin' us in with the cut.

"Right away comes Lord an' Lady ——— to shake hands. But
they didn't introduce us to anybody like we'd 'a done, an' I was
damn glad they didn't. We just milled around a little till we
saw a good place, an' we bedded down there till dinner was
announced.

"Then here comes Lord and Lady ——— lookin' for us again.
The Lord took Mame an' turned the Lady over to me for my
dinner partner. God!" He shuddered, his teeth and fingers clos-
ing a tobacco sack with a jerk as though his thought of the occasion were torturing him. "She was a mighty fine old gal. Me and
her got along good from the jump," he hurried on to say, thinking that I might have misunderstood his shuddering. "Trouble

---

[2] Lord and Lady Ramsay gave the dinner. The story is also told in Adams
and Britzman, *op. cit.,* 204f., but briefly.

was she was Norman built an' never coulda been a high jumper. An' worse'n that, for me, she was adraggin' a train of skirts behind her as long as a stake rope. I saw right away that me an' her couldn't get through the dinin'-room door side by side, so I stepped back a little an' like a damn fool plunked my boot right plumb down on her train. God!" He shuddered again, throwing his ruined cigaret into the lodge fire. "I saw her squat to pull like a cow pony, an' I heard an awful rippin' like tearin' canvas. God! The rest of the way in I walked straddle of her train, feelin' awful."

Much as he liked England, Charley grew homesick there, and his trip to France increased his desire to get home. A mutual friend who entertained him in Paris told me that he tried to induce him to see more of Europe before leaving it.

"Are you going to Rome, Charley?" this friend asked.

"Nope, not me," Charley answered, shortly and positively.

"You should go to Rome, by all means. It's only a step from here, you know. In Rome you would see many of the world's most wonderful paintings and the work of famous sculptors. You might even see the Pope."

"I wouldn't go to Rome to see Christ himself. No sir! I'm goin' back to Montana an' stay there as long as I live."

Santa Barbara, California

DURING the winter of 1922–23 the Lindermans and the Russells were all in Santa Barbara. Our houses were next door to one another on the boulevard near the ocean, so near that breakers occasionally reached our sidewalks. The whistling buoy moaned day and night far out on the endless water. The white surf crashed on the sandy beach ceaselessly.

Through our windows we looked out upon water where the brig *Pilgrim* had anchored so long ago, perhaps while Dana, one of her sailors, wrote chapters of *Two Years Before the Mast*. A near-by bronze tablet recorded that Cabrillo, the Spaniard who perished on San Miguel Island within sight of the tablet, had landed on this spot in 1543. On the beach in great numbers were gulls, pelicans, sanderlings, ducks, and cormorants, and sometimes even curlews, that Charley and I believed must have come down from Montana. Charley and I were entranced by the marvelous fishing of the clumsy-seeming pelicans and the brilliant retreats of squadrons of tiny sanderlings when they were too perilously near breakers. A delightful place, Santa Barbara.

One night a great storm came. Heavy breakers pounded the beach. The gale rocked our houses. The next morning I looked out and saw that not far away was a boat driven ashore by the storm. We needed a boat. I dressed hastily and called Charley. We went out and examined the boat, pods of kelp popping beneath our boots. The boat had never been much of a craft—she was flat-bottomed, poorly modeled, and now badly battered and stove in at the stern. Nevertheless, she was ours by right of salvage, and we dragged her up the beach above high tide and left her to dry out in the sun. We went then on a search for oakum to calk her seams, but not an ounce was to be had in that seaport city.

Our uptown hangout was Ed Borein's studio.[3] Everybody who goes to Santa Barbara goes to native-born Ed either to purchase etchings or to secure needed information. The studio was both a museum and a veritable clearinghouse for transient notables. We asked Ed where we could obtain oakum, just a few ounces, but Ed didn't know.

As he followed us to his door he said, "Say, Frank, there was a swell-looking officer off the battleship *Oklahoma* looking for you this morning. He said he knew you in Helena and wants to see you. Better look him up."

Hah, oakum in the offing! We were on its trail. "What's his name, Ed?"

"Lieutenant Hubbard. The *Oklahoma* is anchored off the pier. He seems like a hell of a good fellow."

"Humph, a sailor from Montana!" growled Charley. "He's a hell of a long way from home. Hosses must be gettin' scarce when Montana boys have to learn to ride battleships."

Within an hour Lieutenant Hubbard was our gracious host, and we were scooting over the waves toward the *Oklahoma* in one of her fast launches. We were shown over the ship and then invited to dine with the Lieutenant and other officers. (On another day Mrs. Linderman, our daughters, and I were entertained in the same delightful manner.)

Oakum had been on my mind ever since leaving Ed Borein's

[3] Ed Borein was a California etcher and painter of the old Western scene. Russell met him in New York City. Linderman met him in Santa Barbara. His sketchbook was edited by Edward S. Spaulding and published by the Edward Borein Memorial Association, under the title *Ed Borein's West* (Santa Barbara, 1952).

studio, and yet I hesitated to mention our need to so gracious a host. Charley's repeated whispering, "Don't forget to hit him for some oakum," embarrassed me. The request seemed inappropriate. So the conversation went on, about the plains and the sea, about horses and ships, all the time taking us farther and farther away from oakum. Evening came. Lieutenant Hubbard and some fellow officers were escorting us to the launch, and we were about to descend into it when Charley reminded me again to "hit him for some oakum." I asked for it, telling him of our need. Immediately the Lieutenant spoke to a sailor, who disappeared into the shadow of a turret as if to show us that the big ship's hospitality was not confined to its officers. Almost immediately he reappeared and handed the Lieutenant a bundle of oakum, its size embarrassing us.

"Wow!" said Charley when we had landed and were walking up the pier, "Our taxidermist pardner Harry Stanford can build us a buffalo with what we don't use."

We calked the boat and mended the stern, but we got little pleasure from the craft. Charley was a poor sailor. "Too much damn water out there," he growled whenever I asked him to go fishing with me. Once, however, when mackerel were running, I induced him to go, but only once.

The day was fine, no wind, no breakers in sight, the blue sea rolling lazily in smooth, dead swells out beyond the kelp beds where we would be fishing. After a long pull we unlimbered our poles, rigged the lines with gangs of ten hooks each, and began to fish. When these fish bite they go after anything, and that day they were biting. They were ravenous. I caught as many as eight at a time on my ten hooks. The beautiful fish piled up in the bottom of the boat and wriggled about our feet.

Suddenly Charley shouted, "Look, what the hell's that? By God, if he comes up under our boat we'll be bait for him. Wow!"

I stood up and saw big sea animals pitching and playing about our boat, so near that we could see their bruised sides. "A school of porpoises, I guess," I said.

Charley had thought the whole school was one big monster.

"You can have my share of this mackerel business an' this damn boat, too," Charley grumbled. His fish-line was zigzagging wildly in the blue water.

"Pull in, Russ, pull in your line; there's fish on your hooks."

His line was cutting in under the boat.

"To hell with 'em. Pull 'em in yourself. I'm plumb full of grub I don't want," he grumbled and draped himself over the boat's stern sick as a dog.[4]

We pulled for the shore. Charley's face was ashen. When we were ashore he asked, "Ever get seasick?"

"No," I said, "but I've known old sailors to get seasick. I once saw a skipper get so sick he had to go below."

"Humph! By God, if I was a sailor that got seasick I'd sure's hell get me a job in Glacier Park."

That winter Santa Barbara was kind to us all. The Linder-mans had reached the city two months before the Russells ar-

---

[4] On the trip to England the ocean was rough, and both Charley and Nancy were seasick—" 'I feel like I swallowed a bull snake, but he won't keep still,' Charlie told his wife." (Adams and Britzman, *op. cit.*, 203.)

rived and had made many acquaintances. At dinners and other social occasions I had told Western stories until I was beginning to repeat some of them. Charley's coming promised relief for both our Santa Barbara friends and me. "Invite the Russells," I urged a lady with whom we were sufficiently acquainted to allow of such a request, "Charley is the best of storytellers."

She did ask the Russells. I shall never forget her astonishment when Charley appeared among her properly attired guests in a tuxedo, with no vest, with his red sash and riding boots.[5] He had gone his limit on dressing up for the occasion, and nobody, not even Mame, could have driven him to greater propriety.

"What perfectly exquisite hands Mr. Russell has," our tactful hostess whispered to me, her keen eyes counting the rings on Charley's fingers.

"They are even more wonderful than they appear," I said, recalling the miracles I had seen them perform. "I'll try to get him started at storytelling, but please don't let anyone ask him for a story outright. Stories have to be suggested by incidents."

I knew from experience that nothing is more difficult than to begin storytelling from a standing start and nothing easier, for a good storyteller, than following up a suggestion. I knew that Charley would balk if asked outright, particularly as he was among strangers.

[5] Linderman states in Chapter IX of this volume that he again and again urged Charley to wear other than cowboy boots but to no avail. Shelton, *op. cit.,* 100, tells of his being given, when living with the Bloods, a pair of beautiful "nicely beaded, lined moccasins," which he slipped his feet into and "for the first time since his arrival in Helena he walked forth in something other than cowboy boots."

Charley had a fondness for French *voyageur* and Indian half-blood dialects, so I told some tales in those dialects and ended by asking Russ if he had known old Becky Sharp.

His eyes lighted and he rubbed his hands together. "Yeah, I knew him. Where'd you know him?" His chuckles engaged the attention of the guests. He began to roll a cigaret. Before I could answer he went on, "Ever know old Becky to take a stand on anything?" Again before I could answer, "No, you never did, nor anybody else."

"Old Becky, Dave Foot, an' big George Long was camped in a wood-hawk's cabin on the Missouri the fall of '83. I was there for a while. They wasn't gettin' along good. They was all cranks. Dave an' Bill kinda had it in for old Becky because he would never take sides in their arguments; he just let 'em alone, pretendin' not to hear 'em at all. 'Course they didn't know it, but old Becky's keepin' out of everythin' they started was all that kept the two of 'em on speakin' terms. It gave 'em somethin' to talk about, an' they sure talked plenty.

"One mornin' when I was there Big George says, 'Dave, I'll bet ye that Navaho blanket o' mine agin yer rifle sling that I can make ol' Becky ante right out straight. I'll bet I can make 'im take a stand fer once in his life.'

"Becky was comin' up from the river with a camp kettle of water. 'You're on, old-timer,' Dave says quick's a wink. 'I always did want that old Navaho blanket o' your'n.'

" 'Yeah, but look here, Dave, ya gotta play up to my lead,' Big George says. 'An' I don't care how strong ya make her play.'

" 'Ya mean I gotta help ya win my rifle sling?' Dave says, nudgin' me.

" 'No, I don't mean that, because if ya make her play strong enough ya might win yaself. Anyway, when I come in tonight you follow my lead, hey?' Dave agrees.

"Old Becky had just lit a candle so's he could see to make some sour-dough bread when Big George sets his rifle in the corner near his bunk.

" 'Git any meat, George?' Dave asks, pourin' some water to wash his hands.

" 'Uh-huh, killed a little buffalo bull. He's fat's butter, too.' George says, strippin' off his buckskin shirt.

" 'Where'd ya find him?'

" 'Down in that cottonwood bottom below here 'bout two mile.'

" 'Humph, funny place to find a buffalo. What ya reckon he was doin' in that thick grove o' trees?' Dave asks, wipin' his hands careful.

" 'Don' know, but when I run onto 'im he was up in the top of a big cottonwood.'

" 'Why, you ol' . . . ,' Dave, glancing at old Becky pattin' a bannock into a fryin' pan, hesitated.

" 'What the hell was he doin' up in that treetop, George?' Dave asks, nudgin' Becky with his elbow.

" 'Eatin' grapes, I guess. Anyway, when he fell 'is mouth was full o' them,' George says, as serious as a kid pullin' out a splinter.

" 'My God, did ya hear that, Becky?' Dave asks.

"Becky stooped to put his bannock before the fireplace. 'I heared 'im. Think I'm plumb deef?' Becky was watchin' his bread, his stumpy fingers spread afore the blaze.

" 'Do ya believe that damn lie?' Dave asks, squattin' beside the old boy an' pointin' over 'is shoulder at Big George.

"Becky loosens his bannock from the pan's bottom with a quick jerk an' twirled it around. An' then he begins to rub the dry dough off'n his fingers like he hadn't heard the question.

" 'Ever hear of a buffalo climbin' a cottonwood tree? Er any other kind a tree?' Dave was pressing his point now, sure of his bet.

" 'N . . . oooo,' old Becky says, like he'd had to fish deep. 'N . . . oooo, I never did. But hell, Dave, ya can't never tell what a young bull'll do when he's after grapes,' he says, floppin' his bannock."

The guests were laughing and Charley knew they wanted another story. They would have got it, anyway. He hardly paused. "One time Dave an' old Becky were out after elk but got mixed up with a buffalo bull. Early in the hunt Becky's horse stepped in a badger hole an' fell an' busted off Becky's rifle stock; but they went on just the same with only one gun. 'Bout noon they run onto plenty of elk signs an' staked their hosses to hunt afoot. Dave walked ahead with the rifle, with old Becky right at his heels. The elk was higher up among scatterin' pine trees that grew just below a long ledge of rock full of holes an' little caves. The trees were far apart.

"Dave an' old Becky followed the elk sign that skirted the

ledge, walkin' careful an' expectin' every minute to get a shot. Both the old boys were lookin' straight ahead when off to one side a noise suddenly warned old Becky. 'Dave! Dave!' he whispers, pointin' to an old buffalo bull that had been horned out of the herd an' was up there alone.

"Of course, he was on the peck. He was not more'n seventy yards away an' was watchin' 'em, his eyes mean as a mad Injin's. Dave cut loose with the gun too quick because he was taken all of a sudden an' made a gut shot that only staggered the bull.

" 'Look out, Dave, look out! He's goin' to charge. Give 'im another, quick, quick!' Becky says.

"Dave tries but the cartridge shell stuck fast in the chamber of his rifle an' he couldn't budge it. An' here come the bull, head down.

" 'Take keer o' yaself,' Dave says to old Becky, droppin' the rifle an' climbing one of them trees that was right beside him.

"Old Becky tried to follow but Dave's heels kicked him in the face an' he looked for another tree, but there warn't none near. 'Whoopee,' he yells an' ducks into a handy hole in the ledge. The mad bull was right at his belt.

"Coonin' his tree to a limb Dave hooked an arm over it to get his breath. He looked down at the rifle an' over at the gut-shot bull that was pawin' shale at the mouth of Becky's hole.

"Dave was an old buffalo hunter an' he could tell the bull was mortal wounded, but he couldn't tell how long the brute would live. He might last till night an' a buffalo bull that is wounded is bad medicine. He wound his legs round the tree trunk and hung on but he was gettin' tired when the old bull grew sick from his wound and began wandering down the hill, his nose 'most draggin' on the ground.

"Right away Dave thought he could get his gun an' get the shell out of its chamber. He let go his hold on the limb an' worked down about ten feet. But he made a little noise an' so when he was about on the ground out pops old Becky from his hole. Wow! the big bull turns an' was after him in a second an' drove him back in his hole an' began pawin' like he did before. 'Course Dave had to coon it back up his tree an' hang on there.

"This time the old bull didn't stay long but staggered off like he was goin' to lay down. Right away Dave begins to slip down the tree once more. His arms an' legs was gettin' mighty tired. When he was about ten feet from the ground out pops old Becky again lookin' wildly round for the bull.

" 'Say, ya damned old fool, don't ya know nothin' at all?' Dave yells, mad's a bald-faced hornet. 'I could come down an' git the rifle an' kill the damned bull if you'd stay in that hole o' yourn.'

" 'Stay in that hole? Hell!' Becky says, lookin' behind him. 'There's a grizzly bear in that hole.' "

On and on went Charley's stories of Montana, different from any the guests had ever heard. He kept them merry for hours. No other man could have told the stories as he did, and even if he learned them word for word he could never have said or written them. He was a master teller.

Mr. F. P. Knott gave a stag dinner in his Montecito home to introduce Charley and me to a group of men we could never forget. A day or two after this dinner Mr. C. K. G. Billings,[6] who had been with us at Mr. Knott's home, invited Charley and me to meet him at his stables, where he wished to "show us some horses he had." Rain was falling when we arrived. Mr. Billings and Mr. Knott met us at the stables door and took us into the vine-covered building. Its long aisle between the horse stalls was carpeted as church aisles are, and the whole interior was neat as a pin. Upon an order from Mr. Billings a wrangler brought out a black gelding. Mr. Billings fondly took the halter from the man's hand and trotted the horse around us. "Uhlan," he said, stopping the animal beside us. "Now watch him. I'm going to give him some sugar and he knows it. If I reach into my pocket after giving him the lump, he will immediately chew and swallow the sugar; but if my hand doesn't reach for my pocket a second time, he will tuck the lump away in his lips and let it slowly melt, thinking he will get no more."

True, all true, but Charley and I saw nothing to rave about in that. The horse was led away and the man brought out a sorrel mare. Mr. Billings trotted her around us. "Lou Dillon," he said, and fondly gave the mare a lump of sugar.

"Fine mare," said Charley.

"Fine mare," I echoed.

These showings went on for some time, and then the wrangler brought out a small cayuse stallion. He was the picture of grace and beauty. Man!

Mr. Billings got praise for his horse now, got plenty of it from

[6] C. K. G. Billings was an Eastern financier who wintered in Santa Barbara.

both Charley and me. Somehow it didn't seem to please him. Even Mr. Knott looked a bit discouraged.

"Well, let's go up to the house," Mr. Billings proposed, as if nothing more were to be had here, and led the way up the hill.

The house was palatial. In it were pictures by Corot, Millet, Innes, Monet, and many other painters. A painting by Rosa Bonheur stopped Charley in his tracks. "By God, I can smell the cows that old gal painted," he said, clearing his throat. "She sure knew her cows an' hosses."

"Let me show you my trophy room," Mr. Billings suggested.

It was in that room that Charley and I, among scores of gold and silver cups and bowls and paintings of horses, began to feel deeply ashamed.

Standing beneath the painting of a wild-looking mare our suffering host said, "That's the mother of Lou Dillon. I searched the United States for that picture. I even employed Pinkerton detectives to run it down. But one day, on a saloon wall up in Montana, I found the painting myself. I shall never forget how tickled I was."

Mr. Knott added, "Royalty in Europe has actually knelt before the great Uhlan, and Lou Dillon is royalty itself." He said this as if he realized that great effort had been wasted on Charley and me.

Now, after all these hours, we understood that we had been seeing the real Uhlan, the real Lou Dillon, the fastest, most famous horses in all the world.[7]

[7] Uhlan was a world-champion trotter from 1912 to 1921. Lou Dillon was the world's first two-minute trotter.

And we had raved over the cayuse stallion, instead!

There was nothing we could do or say now; we were in over our heads. We were glad to get away and try to forget.

"Just the same," Charley chuckled on our way home, "that was a dandy little hoss, that cayuse stud."

"I had to paint," said Charley, and paint he did—before his marriage mostly for fun and food; after marriage for fun and food and lodging and, kept at it by his wife, for fame and fortune. He himself never cared much for the last two, though, being human, he enjoyed them. Mame wanted both, strongly.

Charley also modeled in wax and clay, and later in his career some of his works were cast in bronze. The works of sculpture have received less attention than his paintings, possibly because the latter were more numerous.

Frank Linderman over and over refers to Charley's restless fingers, at work on the lump of beeswax and tallow which he always carried in his pocket and in his war bag. His fingers shaped small animal figures with incredible speed and great likeness and often without sight of what the fingers were doing.

Russell's letters are highly prized, as much, in many instances, for their sketches as for their words and sentiment.

CHARLEY loved beauty. He was always alert to it and recognized it in its faintest line even in crudity itself. Grace, especially in the forms and movements of animals, fascinated him. The colors he used in his paintings were those he saw on men and animals and in landscapes.

He was modest in the extreme about his work. "I ain't an artist," he often reminded me, "I'm an illustrator."[1] But artist or illustrator I believe no greater draftsman than Charley ever lived.

If Russell had not painted pictures the world, I am confident, would have hailed him as its master sculptor of America's native Western animals. In everything he made with his hands, of whatever material, there was always mastery.[2] The natural grace and beauty of his modeled animals amazed naturalists. In modeling, his fingers seemed never for a moment to hesitate. From lumps of clay his animals appeared without effort, as if by magic. Many and many a time I have seen him, while talking and laughing in our camps, cover a piece of modeling wax and his hands

[1] In *Trails Plowed Under*, Charley wrote, "To have talent is no credit to its owner," and in *More Rawhides*, "I am an illustrator. There are lots better ones, but some worse." Russell expressed these ideas many times.

[2] Russell's bronzes have not received the attention that his paintings have. In the spring of 1962 the Kennedy Galleries published a *Sales Catalogue of Bronzes* from the C. S. McNair Collection of Charles Russell Bronzes. It contains sixty-seven excellent pictures of Russell bronzes. In the Foreword, F. G. Renner, of Washington, D.C., writes: "Admirers of Charles Marion Russell have long known him as one of America's finest sculptors and it is not without reason that he has been called Montana's poet laureate in Bronze. Certainly many of his sculptured pieces are sheer poetry in motion."

with his hat and then, without glancing at his work, produce with incredible speed from beneath it a bear, a deer, a pig, a dog.[3]

Charley always carried in his pocket a lump of modeling wax, and always, before our campfires, his long fingers were toying with it as though aching for a commission from their master. Often in his painting when the desired posture of a figure stubbornly refused to submit to his brush he hastily fashioned a clay model that ironed out the difficulties.

"Did you ever use living models, Russ?" I asked him one day when clay had helped him with a picture.

His belly shook with laughter. "A human model would have a hell of a time posin' for me. I'd have to spike him onto a wall. Nope, I get along all right with mud. I don't have to send for it an' it don't cost me anything."

A human model would indeed have found difficulty in posing for Charley Russell. An old cowhand used to say, "Everything Russ paints is agoin' some."

Russell had no experience with watercraft, particularly sailboats, and yet at his cabin on Lake McDonald he made toy schooners and ships that were exquisitely modeled.[4] When he

[3] McCracken, *op. cit.,* 110, quotes a little old lady who lived in Missoula: ". . . he kept grinning at me and talking. . . . he had his hat off and his hands were fumbling around underneath it. . . . in a few moments he put his hat back on and with an even bigger grin he handed me a piece of clay, which he had been modeling out of sight into a funny little girl in a sunbonnet." Shelton writes, *op. cit.,* 35: "In his spare time, Charlie would take a lump of wax and pad and pencil and settle down on some advantageous knoll to copy the animals he saw."

[4] One day when on the ocean front in New York with the actor Bill Hart

sailed them on the lake their rudders were so perfectly controlled by their sails that when set upon a course in a beam wind they kept right to it. He followed his scudding vessels, wading along the lake shore like a small boy. Often, when called to supper, he had to resort to a skiff to recover them.

In the Hopi country the Indian women showed him how they modeled and baked their pottery. Finding suitable clay at Lake McDonald,[5] he modeled Indians, buffalo, horses, and elk and baked his creations Hopi fashion, as though all his life he had worked at pottery-making. "Them old gals savvy mud," he told me once, carefully cooling a baked buffalo.

Charley wanted the country left as the good Lord had made it. Man-made things had little satisfaction for him and often received his disgust. Just so, unnatural objects or processes did not rouse his interest. An amusing incident illustrates this. Once when I was at his Lake McDonald cabin he complained of his wife's bringing several grown hens and a half-dozen chicks to the cabin that had been hatched in an incubator in Great Falls. "This place," he said, "is gettin' more like a farm every day."

and Nancy, Russell "came upon a full-rigged sailing ship moored to the wharf . . . billed for Australia." The captain invited them aboard and told them "salty yarns of the sea all afternoon. . . . When Charlie went back to the studio, he made a model of the ship." The account is in Shelton, *op. cit.,* 151.

[5] McCracken, *op. cit.,* 203f., writes: "In little coves and nooks of the stream near his lake McDonald cabin," which he called Bull's Head Lodge "after the buffalo skull that he always used as a signature on all his paintings, Charlie arranged little groups of miniature figures of Indians, with tiny bows and arrows, horses and tepees, and grotesque little men-of-the-mountains, with beards of moss . . . in clay or carved out of wood."

The chickens, however, recognized a friend in Charley and followed him in a flock wherever he went. One day we started for a tramp in the forest. The chickens trailed us. Of course, if they followed us far into the timber a coyote or a mink or weasel would pick some of them up. Charley turned to frighten the chickens with his hat. "Go back," he commanded, but so kindly that the chickens only stared at him and edged a little closer. "Go back," he said, more sharply, throwing a tiny dry stick at the flock. The chickens rushed into a quarrelsome huddle over the harmless missile. One of the hens seized a small chick by the toe, making it flutter its stubby wings frantically and cry out. "Did you see that?" Charley asked, incredulously. Quick anger showed in his eyes. "By God, she was tryin' to eat the toes off that little chick. Yes sir, she was. Get out of here, you unnatural bitch," he cried hotly, hurling a stone at the hen. "I bet *your mother* was a damned coal oil lamp, too." He turned to me, "If these smart fellers don't quit foolin' with things tryin' to beat God Almighty at His own game," he declared bitterly, "we'll all be tryin' to eat each other one of these days just like that damned incubator hen."

But getting back to painting, Charley recognized skill and truth in the work of any artist or craftsman. For instance, Oriental art, even those pieces hastily made to sell at low prices, interested him deeply. Japanese painting or brasswork or particularly wood carvings he would look at admiringly. "You'd think a beaver gnawed some of 'em out," he chuckled one day when we were looking at them. "Nobody does 'em like they do. They've got somethin' that nobody else has got." He paused meditatively.

"I guess peacocks belong in India but just the same every time I see a peacock I think of a Chinaman painter. I'd sure like to see their country."

Some time later when we were looking at some beautiful ring-necked pheasants, the colors of the cock's feathers glinting and changing in the sunlight, Charley, scarcely breathing, walked slowly round and round the wire enclosure. "Don't they look like a Chinaman made 'em?" he asked, his eyes dancing. Again he said, "I'd sure like to see their country."

Once he spoke feelingly of Indian painting: "You hear say an Injin can't paint; but just the same you never have to wonder what an Injin tried to draw. His hosses look like hosses an' his buffalo look like buffalo. An' just look what an Injin can do with colors! Nobody else can do things with color like he can. I can't, anyway."

He hated the counterfeit of anything and could not pose.[6] Sham or what he believed to be sham in the work of an artist disgusted him. Yet, though he knew he could speak freely with me, I heard him only once disparage the work of fellow artists, and then he confined his criticism to a particular school of artists, mentioning no individual.[7] At that time he was showing me his

[6] This line has been taken from Linderman's article upon Russell's death in *The Outlook,* Vol. CXLV (April 13, 1927), 466–68.

[7] "Had you questioned him [Russell] concerning his artistic aspirations, he would have given a deprecatory smile and said, 'Naw, them artist fellers study in Europe and around and they paint with what they call technique. Me, I just try to record some of the things I've seen, here and there." (Shelton, *op. cit.,* 114.) No assertion is made that he actually spoke these words—as occurs in many places in this biography. The ideas would belong probably to the

paintings made since my last visit to the studio. Finally, he drew a canvas from behind several that were leaning against the wall. "That," he said, "is the last one." He turned his back toward me and rolled a cigaret. The picture was unlike anything that had ever come from his brush. I knew now why he had turned his back on me. The coloring was strange; the landscape was dim; the figures were scarcely discernible. The picture had nothing for me.

"Uh-huh," he said, without turning around, "you don't like the picture." He now turned to face me. "That's because you *cahn't* appreciate true *aht.*" He stooped beside the picture, anger coming over him.

"Look—these are cows," his fingers brushed the canvas, "an' that's a water hole, an' this is a cowpuncher. Yeah, I know, but dust *obscuahs* 'em so's you wouldn't know what they are. But *I* know, because I put 'em there myself." He hurried on, "It's an impressionistic pictuah," he said, bitterly sarcastic. "Know why painters are impressionistic? 'Cause they can't draw an' they know they can't. So they blur their paintin' an hide their bum drawin.' Just let your eyes try to follow a man's leg that they draw; start from the boot—the leg's as likely to run into his belly as anywhere else. Hell!"

---

period around 1890. In *The Anaconda Standard* for December 15, 1901, quoted in McCracken, *op. cit.,* 187, Charley said, "I was down to St. Louis and I had a chance to see what Easterners like. They are all daft on the impressionistic school. In one gallery I saw a landscape they were raving about. Color! Why, say, if I ever saw colors like that in a landscape I would never take another drink. A man who would paint such a thing and represent it as a copy of nature must be on the ragged edge."

He looked loathingly at his picture. "That's an ordered picture. A man wants it, but he ain't goin' to get it." He turned and deliberately kicked a hole in the canvas.

I had never seen Charley in such a mood, but it lasted only a few seconds. "Mebby," he said humbly, "Mebby they've got something I can't see. An' anyway, they got to live."

Charley's appreciation of the work of other artists was genuine and generous. No one felt more elation than he when I succeeded in getting a landscape by Ralph DeCamp[8] permanently hung above the mantel in the card room of the Montana Club in Helena. "That old boy," he said to me one morning when I found him looking at a DeCamp in our living room here at Goose Bay, "That boy can sure paint the wettest water of anybody I know. You can hear his rivers ripple. Frank, that's a good picture," he went on, stepping back and squinting his eyes to look at it again.

"Yes," I said, "we are all fond of that picture. I wish, though, that the doe on the sandbar didn't have that white spot on her forehead. It makes her look bald-faced."

"It's the light. See, it comes . . ."

"I know," I interrupted, "but I wish that sometime when you are here you'd paint out that white spot. Ralph wouldn't care; I know he wouldn't."

Charley made no reply, but he shook his head.

That afternoon when I returned from Somers he had not only

[8] Ralph DeCamp (1853–1936) was a landscape painter in oils who lived in Helena from 1886 to 1935. Ten of his paintings are in the Law Library in the State Capitol Building in Helena.

93

painted out the objectionable spot on the doe's forehead but the doe herself and had painted in a doe of his own with two fawns behind her, so that now there are three Charley Russell deer on a Ralph DeCamp sandbar here at Goose Bay. In this I am certain that our picture is unique.

Later, when Ralph DeCamp visited us I showed him what Charley had done, feeling a bit skittish as he walked slowly toward the picture. "You aren't hurt by it, Ralph?" I asked, worried by his silence.

"Hurt," he exclaimed, turning on me sharply. "Hurt by it? Hell no. It's made me proud." He laughed, his blue eyes happy as a boy's.

Both of these men who did so much for Montana are now camped on some showery cloud. Charley led the older Ralph into the shadows by ten years.

Of all the pictures he ever painted I believe that the canvas above the mantel in the reading room of the Montana Club at Helena gave Charley the most trouble. The scene is an immense herd of buffalo crossing the Missouri River.[9] A huge bull is in the foreground on the very spot where Charley and I once camped. This bull delayed for three months (in 1915) the delivery of the picture.

[9] Nancy Russell wrote to Linderman on January 27, 1914: "Chas has lots to do on the buffalo picture [for the Montana Club] but it is just coming along fine. It is the most peaceful thing and that dear old river, you sure will like it. I have ordered a hundred dollar frame for it, does that start to take your breath? Now honest Injun do you think there will be a bunch at that club have heart failure?" Letter in the care of Norma Linderman Waller, Kalispell.

The fussy chairman of the Club's Board of Governors warned me when I secured this commission for Charley, "Now, Frank, get him once in his life to paint something that is standing still. I cannot live in a room with the usual Russell paintings, they make me nervous."

As a dutiful member of the famous old Club I transmitted this warning to Charley, and it was this and nothing else that caused the trouble. Charley simply could not make the big buffalo bull stand still. I saw him myself paint a dozen bulls into the picture. I feel certain that fifty bulls must have temporarily led that painted herd before the picture reached the reading room.

"Had to fight hell out of that damned bull," Charley told me disgustedly.

I took the picture from his studio in Great Falls and carried it in my hands to and from the train and to the Club. I hung it above the mantel, and I shall never forget my effort to get a good light on the painting. I wanted the Board, of course, to view the painting at its best advantage. I was ready to bristle at the smallest unfavorable comment on Charley's work.

I had no financial interest in the picture's acceptance. I simply wanted the satisfaction of having served both my friend and my Club, and yet for days pending the Board's decision I was as touchy as a porcupine. Late in the afternoon of the momentous day not more than an hour before the Board's final meeting I was in the reading room with two of the Governors when one of the older members entered. He had once been a Governor and felt his importance. Pompous as a strutting turkey cock, he adjusted his pince-nez to inspect the painting from behind us. "Humph!" he snorted, tumbling the pince-nez from his nose to dangle on its black ribbon, "Humph! That's a miserable bull in the foreground. Humph!" He strutted from the room, his thumping cane expressing his disgust.

I was worried. But the Board accepted the picture and I heard no other unfavorable comment.[10] Nevertheless, because the big bull *was* the picture I could not forget the pompous member's comment. I told Charley, even though I knew the man's narrow criticism would sting him a little.

"Miserable bull, hey?" he muttered and put down his anger by clearing his throat. "Well, mebby he is a bum bull, all right, but he's the best buffalo bull I ever painted just the same."

Considerable opposition existed to Charley's painting the huge mural behind the Speaker's station in the House of Representatives in the capitol building in Helena.[11] The Board that con-

[10] On January 15, 1915, Nancy Russell wrote to Linderman: "We are so pleased to know that the Club members like their picture. You have done almost the impossible in arousing so much enthusiasm." Again on January 19, 1915: "The check for $500 [the down payment; the total price was $3,000] and the notes with the agreement from the Montana Club received. . . . We thank you for this whole business because it would never have gone through without you." Letter in the care of Norma Linderman Waller, Kalispell.

[11] Adams and Britzman, *op. cit.,* go not much beyond description of the mural. Shelton, *op. cit.,* 190–92, has an account different from Linderman's. Austin Russell's account is again different (*op. cit.,* 225–27): "Charlie had to go to Helena and appear in person before the Senate and fight to get the contract. His argument ran, 'If you want cupids and angels and Greek goddesses, give this New Yorker [John Alexander] the job. If you want a western

trolled the disposal of the five-thousand dollar contract consisted of the Governor, the Secretary of State, and the Attorney General. Many times it was warned against employing an inexperienced artist. Charley had never painted a mural, and the Board, for that reason, tended to lean away from giving him the commission. The Secretary of State, however, whose deputy I was, championed Charley from the beginning of the controversy. As his deputy I was acting as Secretary of State in his absence; I had no vote on standing committees or boards upon which he was a member, and therefore I feared final action might be taken on the commission and I would be powerless to keep it from being given to an experienced Eastern artist who had been haunting the capitol. Fortunately, the Secretary, A. N. Yoder, returned to his office in time to attend the important meeting at which the commission was to be voted. Finally, in July, 1911, the Board unanimously selected Charley to paint the picture. I was deputized to carry the news to him in Great Falls.

I was bubbling over with joy when I reached his home; but if Charley felt any thrills, he did not show them. He did not even

picture, give it to me.' This was a real ordeal to Charlie, who hated to brag about his work or disparage another painter." McCracken, *op. cit.,* 209–10, calls the mural "one of the finest examples of Western American art." He states that Mrs. Russell received a letter dated June 26, 1911, from Governor E. L. Norris requesting Russell to appear before the State Board of Examiners on June 30, "relative to executing of a large historical mural painting" for the House of Representatives, a picture which had been under consideration for "at least two years." On July 3, Governor Norris stated that the Board "had decided to commission Russell to execute the painting, for the sum of $5,000." The subject was to be Lewis and Clark meeting the Flathead Indians at Ross's Hole.

clear his throat as he habitually did when he was emotionally stirred.

This was his first mural, his first large painting, his first big money. During the whole evening he was unusually quiet, seldom speaking, not once sketching for the proposed work, as was his wont. Later, I knew that his mind had been engaged on the necessary changes that would have to be made in his studio. Mainly, it would need to be considerably enlarged to accommodate the canvas for the mural. His thoughts that evening had depressed him, for he loved his studio as it was.

When at last the studio had been enlarged and the immense canvas was in place, the shack seemed to me better than before. It bore, however, the appearance of having been cleared for a major battle. Much of its old atmosphere, of course, had been lost forever. This nobody could have felt as keenly as Charley.

His beginning on the mural must have been difficult, yet the picture grew rapidly. It reached completion within the specified time. And what a picture it is!

While Charley was at work upon the painting the weather was exceptionally warm and dry. An electric fan was set up to keep him comfortable as he painted. One day when I had been watching him paint for several hours the shack was as quiet as a cemetery. An occasional passage of words between us and the hum of the fan were the only noises. Yet I grew vaguely conscious of a laborer's work on the street in front of the studio. The blows of his pick against the hardpan reached me. I had seen him as I had arrived, but I had become absorbed in watching Charley paint and had forgotten him.

"Hear that, Frank?" Charley asked. He moved out of the fan's draft to roll and light a cigaret. "Shut that damn thing off," he said, nodding toward the fan. When he spoke again I realized that he too had been hearing the blows of the laborer's pick and that they had bothered him. "Things ain't fair by a damn sight," he said more to himself than to me. Then he turned to face me, "That poor devil out there in the hot sun with the sweat runnin' down his back can't save as much as I'm gettin' for this picture in his whole lifetime, not if he works every day. He's probably got a woman and some kids, too. Here I am sittin' in the shade with an electric fan blowin' on my neck gettin' five thousand dollars for this thing. An' I didn't make the canvas, an' I didn't make the paint, an' I didn't make the brushes. I didn't make a damn thing I'm usin' to make that money with. I just bought 'em with money I made by usin' stuff that other men made for wages—an' damn poor wages, too. By God, that man out there ought to hate me. I wouldn't blame him a damn bit if he walked in here an' killed me with his pick." His voice was scarcely audible; his eyes were troubled.

For some minutes he was silent, then he burst out, "But I plumb had to paint. I'd have been dead long ago if I couldn't have painted. An' that's sure as hell."

There was another pause. "But that man out there couldn't savvy that, an' by God, I don't neither."

He felt a bit relieved. "Here, grab a brush an' help me make this hay," he said jokingly and began painting the grass in the picture's foreground. I set the fan going again.

Painting this large mural gave him little trouble—none at all compared to his distress when, necessarily present at a joint session of the House and the Senate, he was requested to reply to a formal speech of congratulatory acceptance of the picture. He stampeded for the door, frightened. He was literally dragged to the Speaker's station by laughing friends. It was a terrible ordeal for him. As he stood there his mouth opened once or twice but uttered no sound—none, at least, that reached me; his right arm and then his left made one quick, restricted gesture each; and then, with an embarrassed nod to the cheering audience, he bolted. The mural belonged to the state of Montana.

"Did you know they was goin' to do that?" he demanded of me in the lobby, an angry light in his eyes now the exact color of a wolf's.

"No," I said emphatically. And how glad I was that I could truthfully say so!

The two comrades had been happy together on many hunting trips. In the autumn of 1925 they had their last one. It was not a pleasant jaunt, except in the sense of comradeship. They really were, as Russell said, too old for the hardships which the open country and weather put upon campers. Linderman was fifty-six years of age, Russell sixty-one. But the moonlight still delighted them, as did the sheen on the frying pan, the shape of the deer's head. The spirit was still willing but the flesh was weak.

I was watching for the stage on the hillside road behind our home at Goose Bay expecting printer's proof. I was a hundred yards down the trail toward home when I heard the stage stop, but because of thick timber and brush I did not know that it had brought me company until I saw Charley coming down the hill with his rifle, grip, and our mail sack.

"How," he greeted me, dropping the grip to shake hands. He looked along the trail, "Wow! she's plated with gold." He stooped beside the deer trail that cut across the way to home and with his long, many-ringed fingers stirred the yellow tamarack that had carpeted it. He rose and his eyes followed the deer trail, "Headin' straight for the lake," he said wistfully. Makes a feller want to foller it, don't it? Makes him wish he'd been an Injin a hundred years ago."

I followed him along the home trail.

"Got an idea, Frank; let's us take our rifles, a blanket apiece, a little grub and a lot o' salt in packs on our backs an' then let's us strike out west from your back door an' keep goin' till we kill a deer an' then let's us eat him right where he falls. By God, I'll stump you."

I agreed readily, "Good; we'll eat a bite, make up our packs and light out."

"What time is it?" he asked, looking up through the treetops. "But we don't give a damn about the time, do we," he amended, chuckling. "When night comes on we'll camp, meat or no meat. An' then when mornin' breaks we'll go on an' keep goin' till we kill. Wow!"

102

I had never seen Charley happier or more eager to be in the forest. He caught a glimpse of Mrs. Linderman and the girls, who were watching our approach, and waved his hat.

"Been readin' a book about the Eskimos, Frank. They got us beat a Mormon mile. You oughta read that book. When a big whale drifts ashore up in their country they don't fool around havin' him moved, no sir—they just tell their women to move their village to the whale, an' then they eat him up right where he lays. That's what we'll do, by God. We'll kill a deer an' eat him right where he falls. Wow!"

This borrowed idea possessed him so thoroughly that within an hour we were heading westward through the deep forest with our packs on our backs. The November day was perfect, the blue sky like crystal, the sun warm. We tramped and tramped, stopping on high open points to look around and get our wind. The indigo lake far below was shimmering in the sunlight.

When we had gained the top of a steep hill Charley was panting. "I ain't much good any more. I walk like the pigeon-toed fat woman in the circus, an' my hind wheels don't track, an' my old tom-tom goes lickety-split when I climb."

Charley had never been a good walker. No cowboy was. Nothing could induce him to wear shoes or moccasins, even in timber. "If you'd shed those cork-heeled boots, you'd be better off in this kind of country," I said for the fortieth time, and as usual he paid no heed to the advice. I might as well have spoken to the sky. Charley's boots and red sash were as much a part of him as his nose and ears.

The sun had slipped below the treetops, and the air was chilling noticeably and fast when I shot a yearling white-tailed buck dead in his tracks.

"He's just our size, Russ, if we're going to eat him right here." I set to dressing the deer, smiling over our trip.

"Yep, he's plenty big enough, I guess." Charley grinned, squatting beside the buck to sketch its head in the half light. He turned the head every way, his pencil was flying over the paper.

No other man alive knew the anatomy of our native animals as he did, and yet during all the years we had hunted together he never once failed to sketch the bodies, heads, legs, eyes, and ears of deer, elk, bear, mountain sheep, or goats as soon as the animals were dead. None was ever old to him; each seemed to offer something new for his pencil. Inordinately fond of their meat as he was, I never knew him to kill a deer, elk, or any other animal.

"Fat, ain't he?" He posed a hind leg for a quick sketch.

"Yep; but we can't eat him here; there's no water."

"That's right," he agreed. "How far we got to go for water?"

I looked about and took bearings. "About a mile and a half as the crow flies."

"By God, I wish I was a crow. My heels are plumb blistered." He took a few crippled steps, "An' my legs are stiff."

I skinned out a ham and then we legged it through the twilight to water, striking the creek, that grumbled among wide-branched balsam firs, after dark. In such a place we could not hope to find dry wood. On a sweltering August afternoon the spot would have been well enough, but on this cold November evening it was not inviting. Its only level space was matted with frosty leaves and dead ferns.

We hastily broke dry twigs off dead branches and chose a spot for the fire. Charley started the fire and I, knowing that if we left the deer, coyotes would be likely to eat it, began on the backward trail to pack in our meat.

"Will there be a moon?" he called, his breath white in the light of the sickly blaze of the tiny fire.

"You bet, and a big one, too. Better cut a lot of boughs for our bed. We'll need them, Russ."

I shall never forget that night. Our wood would not burn; our meat would not cook; Charley had gathered only a hatful of boughs for our bed. Unable to coax a decent blaze from our campfire, we bedded down early.

The moon came up big as the sky; the matted leaves and dead ferns about us sparkled with frost; every fir needle and every tiny twig stood out against the moon like a fish pole.

"By God, if sleepin' on a bed of diamonds counts any, our line's royal both ways from the deuce." Charley shivered and tucked the blankets about his shoulders. "Damned if a buffalo gnat couldn't look bigger'n a grizzly bear up on that treetop."

We could not get warm. Charley could not lie still. His mind was stimulated by our surroundings. "Wonder how so many colors can get into frost out of moonlight. That little spot by the fryin' pan's got an opal cheated a Mormon mile." He was sitting up and looking around.

"Borrows them from the campfire," I reminded him.

"Yeah, mebby, I didn't think of that. We ought to take the damned fire to bed with us and try to keep warm. An' say, if you'd just lay still, we'd get warm a lot quicker."

"*I* lie still?" I was half angry. "It's you that's doing the fidgeting. Good Lord, I'd as soon sleep with a live bobcat as you. Here we are with two twelve-pound, four-point Hudson's Bay blankets and we can't keep warm on dry ground. If each of us had wrapped up in one of them, as we should have done . . ."

"Hell, pardner, that ain't what's the matter," Charley cut me off, "we're gettin' old. We ain't worth a tinker's damn any more. That's what's the matter. 'Tain't our bed ground nor the weather, it's just us." He lay still for a moment, "By God, I'm goin' straight back to your shack soon's it's light enough to see." He tried to roll a cigaret with his numb fingers.

"What? How about this deer we're going to eat?" I too, however, was thoroughly sick of our trip.

"To hell with him. Let's pack him in to your shack where we can eat him in comfort."

"Right," I said.

There was silence for a few moments, then he broke out again, "Look! Look at that lance of moonlight jabbin' holes in that black water. Wow! If a man could paint that they'd call him a liar."

The following autumn when Mrs. Linderman and I stopped in front of Ed Borein's studio in Santa Barbara after driving down from Montana, a newswoman stepped up to me as I got out of the car.

"Aren't you Mr. Linderman?" she asked, her pad and pencil at ready.

"Yes," I said, wondering what she could want of me.

"Have you heard about Charley Russell?"

"No." My stomach grew cold.

"He's dead," she said.[1]

---

[1] "There can never be another Charley Russell any more than there can be another new Northwest; and if the men of the old days who have left us have kindled their fires in the Shadow Hills, then Russell has found them, and is happy there." (Linderman, *The Outlook, loc. cit.*) Charley Russell died on October 24, 1926.

A GALLERY OF RUSSELL DRAWINGS

III

From *Indian Why Stories*

From *Indian Why Stories*

Courtesy of Dr. Van Kirke Nelson

From *Indian Why Stories*

From *Indian Old-Man Stories*

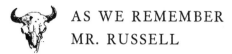

AS WE REMEMBER
MR. RUSSELL

BY WILDA LINDERMAN[1]

CHARLEY RUSSELL's name and a train ride are inextricably associated in my mind. Whether my father and Charley had met at that time and occasioned a discussion of him I do not know. Be that as it may, in my memory we are returning from the ninth state legislature to Sheridan in Madison County, Montana. It is evening, the car is lamp-lighted, a little crowded with other returning legislators, and there is the smell of soot. I look off toward the lights of East Helena and back to my grandmother Linderman's mink collar on her handsome tweed coat. We have been with her that day to have our pictures taken. My gaze returns to the box pleats of my brown dress. I am aware, too, that I am still wearing my best satin ribbons. I feel for the usual curl coming over each shoulder. Why do I persistently associate this scene and its details with the name of Charley Russell? Why should I? It must be that I first heard of him then, and that he had come to have a particular significance for my father at that time. I cannot think otherwise. It is entirely possible, I think, that the idea of placing a historical

[1] Wilda Linderman, the eldest daughter, was graduated from Montana State University in 1921. After teaching school in Santa Barbara, California, for some years and other years in Eastern schools, she set up The Gosling School in Peterborough, New Hampshire. At first the school was only for pre-kindergarten children, but it has expanded to cover later years and has carried some students through the high-school years. She has been owner and headmistress since about 1940.

picture by Charley Russell in the Montana State Capitol which we were leaving may have come to my father at this time.[2]

There must have been further references to Charley in the period before 1908 and 1909. He became an actual figure to me, however, at the time my father was discussing purchase of one of his paintings for the Montana Club—an enthusiasm about which there were differing points of view, I became aware, when his more ardent campaign for a commission for Charley to paint the large historical scene that had been his dream to hang in the capitol in Helena became as intense and against the current of opinion as were his crusades in behalf of the Chippewa and Cree Indians. My father, with some aid of other devotees, won. The painting hangs in proud esteem in that honored building.

Before this period, as I have said, Charley Russell had been but a name. My father wished he could show my mother Charley's best paintings—they were owned by saloons and hung there where they had paid for Charley's drinks, in the days before he had met Mame and married her. Someday—it remained a vague possibility—we might see Charley's best; father wished it could be *now*.

Recollections of Charley Russell for me ever since their inception have gone pretty much along with my life. It is not

[2] Linderman wrote to Russell on September 2, 1916, that had he been elected to the U.S. House of Representatives in this year (he was defeated by Jeannette Rankin), one of his chores would have been "to get a Russell picture in the national capitol or about it somewhere." Charley wrote humorously about the women taking over. Letters among the Linderman Estate materials.

alone that his letters to my father and the original of the cover of my father's first book, *Indian Why Stories,* have hung continuously on the paneling of the walls of my study ever since they left the walls of Goose Bay, our home on Flathead Lake, Montana, or that I have read aloud to the children of Gosling, my own school (named for Goose Bay), my father's legends, and that the conceptions of its characters and settings in Charley's illustrations are an integral part of them—*they* have helped vitally of course, keeping both men alive before us—but that Charley as a person had a real place in the lives of all three of us. My sisters and I each had our own separate discovery of this delightful, originally imaginative, rare person, and responded to his friendship in our own particular ways.

We shared in common a love for Nature, love for the legendary and mythical, a knowledge of the Indians, degrees of desire for creative expression, and appreciation of members of our families.

For my sister Verne, there were perhaps the greatest number of matching facets of their separate natures. Both of them had keen awareness of fashion, of the season's silhouette; for trends of all sorts, the popular as well as the classic; for the comic: the sense of humor of both of them could find expression in cartooning—and *did*—at the expense of all of us, though never unkindly.

Charley appreciated, as my father did, my sister Norma's physical beauty, her nimble hands and feet, the quick translation of her thought into action against my sister Verne's and my own necessity to mull things over—we have always had to *think first*.

Charley Russell liked my own feeling for children and my

ability to interpret them. I have a sweet memory of standing on the dock near his Lake McDonald home, with shadows of the mountains long and pointed on the water, and the atmosphere of the eerie creatures, as of *A Midsummer Night's Dream,* which Charley fashioned of bearded moss and bark all about his cabin woods. Mrs. Russell was there, with Jack in her arms and facing over her shoulder—after the manner of mothers and children of all ages—toward us.

Jack was their two-year-old adopted son for whom my father had been named godfather at his christening, and an absorbing interest of this period. Charley turned to me: "The little fellow saw me in my bathing suit the other day," he said. "I was kind of white where the line of my shirt collar ends. 'Daddy,' he says, 'Daddy, you look *newer* there.'"

"It's fun to read to him," he told me at another time. "Jack likes to be read to, especially *Daffy Down Dilly.* 'Daffy-down-dilly,' he says, 'with a *nello* gowne.' It's a good name for the gowne —*nello* expresses it."

Charley reveled in the films and liked the film stars of his day. He and Nancy knew personally a number of them, and liked to tell about them. Charley would recount in detail and at full length, it seemed to me, a recent movie in which Mary Pickford or Douglas Fairbanks had leading roles, spurred on by my sister Verne, or out of pity for our benighted state as babes in the woods. My sisters Verne and Norma listened enthralled, while I gave only tolerant attention to the narrative; I was more intrigued with Charley's undeniable interest in the plot and his unselfish desire to entertain us than in the plays themselves, which often were pretty poor. Charley had the kind of open-mindedness that could entertain divergent and even conflicting standards. He let in, and allowed them to govern not only his thoughts but actions, often irreconcilable political and religious outlooks and personal viewpoints. There seemed a feeling at times, perhaps amounting almost to a fear, that if he did not he might miss the way, and so he must let them *all* in. This does not discount in the least the fact that he genuinely enjoyed the dramas which he recounted from the screen, usually while he helped with the after-dinner ritual of dishwashing, standing with the three of us by the long light-wood table through the middle of the kitchen, in his inevitable high-heeled boots, facing the driveway up the hill and that western sky that was an unfailing promise at the close of each day—and of which I am sure he was not unmindful—in front of us.

Charley exhibited in Chicago, the year I was a freshman at Northwestern University—at the O'Brien Gallery, I think. My memory, strangely enough, is not importantly of the pictures, but rather of a juxtaposition of their wild action with the Tipperary hats on display then in the Michigan Avenue shop windows and also of gleams of late February sunlight on the wet pavements, the latter two making one almost heady with a premature feeling of spring.

It must be said in the interests of truthfulness that at this period in my life I did not wholly share my father's enthusiasm for Charley and Mame, or Nancy, as she later was known—particularly Nancy, who deviated considerably from the canons of my dancing-school crowd and who never failed to bring a conflict of loyalties into my fairly simple world when, for my father's sake, I tried to like her. It was not until later, on the occasion of a small party which my mother gave for her in Helena, where we had gathered around a table afterward for a second cup of coffee and Nancy revealed a real self there within her which is in us all, that I began to make actual contact with her, and find qualities I could sincerely admire, which outweighed our very different upbringing.

On one of the early exhibition days, my father's brother, Percy Linderman, devoted always to any interest that was my father's, gave a luncheon for Charley and Mame. A cousin of Charley's was one of the guests. I was fascinated, I remember, with his resemblance to Charley. He was younger. (My memory may not serve me correctly, and he might have been a nephew.) He had the same sandy coloring, the same slender hands and feet, and though his bone structure was finer, they were remarkably like. Charley had fine-boned hands and feet and innumerable fine lines crossing and recrossing his face, but Charley's face at this period was broader and his body heavier, perhaps from inactivity as much as anything. He disliked walking always, and rode a horse if he could, causing his movements on his feet, though never self-conscious, to be slightly labored. He had the cowboy's natural pride in small feet, and the high-heeled boots he always wore, which were a very part of him, inhibited his walking. There were additional reasons of health, too, I suspect, as time went on, but at the period of which I now write, the boots probably were the main reason. Charley wore those boots always, even with a tuxedo!

He and my father both, too, wore *ceintures,* the wool woven sashes of the *voyageur.* I never saw Charley without a sash. He even had a cerise silk one for dress occasions. No black-clothes affair was too formal for Charley to preclude the sash, the boots, and the cowboy hat.

The winter our two families were in Santa Barbara, California, in neighboring houses, facing the sea at the point where the wedge of park on Cabrillo Boulevard began, these sashes and the cowboy hats and—for Charley, the cowboy boots—were a familiar sight, for the two men walked on the beach every morning, preceded by our collie, Kim, tawny as they with their sandy complexions and their buckskin coats. My father usually took another walk in the afternoon after his second writing period, but for Charley the morning exertion was sufficient.

On one occasion, Jack, their seven-year-old son, was lost after dark. Charley was agitated but ineffectual, and it was my father who came on the narrow cinder edge of the pavement at long last, holding Jack's hand tightly and narrowly escaping a hit from speeding cars, or so it seemed to his agonized wife and daughters watching them. My father had found Jack in a railroad roundhouse, and needless to say Charley was everjoyed and properly grateful; also, he was touchingly anxious that Jack should not be disciplined, as Nancy was inclined to feel strongly that he should be.

My fondest and most poignant memories of all of Charley are the November visits he made us at Goose Bay. My father and two sisters and I would rise in the early morning. My father would take my mother's breakfast tray in to her beforehand, and we four would eat in the dining room together by candlelight, watch the dawn come, and by the time our old Studebaker was on the drive, the gold of the tamaracks on all of the drives and on our own paths through the woods would be plainly visible. Hoar frost would lie over all the landscape like white-haired age. One picked out the red berries on the long woody stems of kinnikinnick and the blue on the holly-shaped leaves of Oregon grape—a regular rite—and noted the intense stillness of the woods, sometimes broken by a scolding pine squirrel. Those were the days before heated cars. The fact that we shivered a little from cold and drew close to one another for warmth under the blue Indian blanket and could see one another's breath added to the excitement of our being on the way to meet Charley.

On one of these occasions the train was ahead of schedule, and when we got to the Somers station, there was Charley's yellow-tan cowhide bag, with its brass buffalo skull and knobs for trappings, already set down on the platform and Charley himself standing with his great sheep-lined coat wide opened, his cowboy hat on the back of his head, the invariable lock of graying sandy hair down the middle of his forehead, looking for all the world like a child escaped from grown-ups quite un-buttoned-up.

"How!" "How!" the two men met, as though there was nothing unusual in being set down on the platform ahead of your host's arrival.

"Find me a ball gaoun, Gals, find me a ball gaoun," Charley would say as he came in the back door at Goose Bay later on, and as though there had been no interruption of painting from preceding years.

We would seek out Mother, and she would protest that she had few fashion books, since she no longer made little girls' dresses, but in the end she remembered that she had bought a *McCall's* or a *Pictorial Review* for a continued story she was reading, or my sister Verne would produce a current *Vogue* magazine. I think that Charley usually followed the more popular ladies' magazines, rather than *Vogue*.

Usually these painting sprees were in the late afternoon. Sometimes Charley would sit down at my sister Verne's table in front of the open fire, and taking up *her* brushes and dipping into *her* paints go on with a paper doll or Christmas card she had begun. "Wow!" he would protest, "I can't paint children. Every time I paint a little girl she looks a hundred years old."

"And I can't do grown-ups!" my sister would counter. "They always come out like children." It was true, what they both said of their creative efforts. They would laugh together.

Once they conceived the idea of using maple leaves for place-card ladies' skirts. I remember they went out under the November moon and gathered attire from the moose-maple clump in the oval center of our drive. Little gusts of wind would come up and sweep them out of their hands. I remember their laughter, and how my father loved the idea when they brought them in finally to the lamp-lighted, fire-lighted room and deposited them on the paint table for another round of place cards.

Charley's ladies were never to get away from being a little raw-boned. I have a cartoon of his on my walls this moment, a documentary drawing he did for my father of Miss Montana, Uncle Sam, and a Land Hog. Miss Montana wears the most correct hobble skirt of her day, her muff and plumed hat and furs are all that the period decreed, but her face and figure fall short of the femininity that Charley was seeking.

Charley had been deeply concerned when we had moved from Helena to Goose Bay. He was sure that we were going to starve, and he disapproved of my father's taking three "young ladies" into the wilderness. He would come over from his camping place on our Point, as though to cheer us up, and say, "Well, how's all the Swiss Family Robinson this mornin'?"

I cannot recall whether it was on this early November visit, or on a later one that same fall—it seems nearer Christmas, in retrospect—that Charley in the role of cheer-bringer elected to teach my sisters and me the fox trot, the new dance of that season. My sister Verne had had a party hat with navy velvet broad brim and purple felt overlay her freshman year at the University. The hat had a small, flat crown with purple ribbon band and antennae-sort of ends, very chic, where they came together in front. She also had, providentially, a white fox fur neckpiece.

For the fox-trot lesson, and also still to cheer us, Charley donned the fur neckpiece and hat. Then, catching up my sister Norma, called "Babe," he went the length of the long living room and back in his high-heeled boots, red sash, and the absurd hat and neckpiece several times.

The fine lines of his broad face under that incongruous hat seemed more numerous. The mouth and eyes narrowed with cunning—Charley always made himself like the animals he was modeling, and he did likewise for the dance. The red sash flipped rhythmically; the cowboy high-heels were as usual a little awkward as he trotted back and forth. One could not deny, however, an unmistakable fox-feeling about Charley. He captured the spirit of things always.

There were mildly disconcerting moments on occasion. Charley and my father each believed himself a connoisseur of coffee-making—neither, unfortunately, liked the other's brew. It came to a point where, in order to have the coffee right, the two men were vying with one another in early rising.

One morning Charley made perfectly certain of a good cup of coffee by beginning his day—and ours—at four-thirty in the morning. My father was slightly annoyed, as he heard lifting of the lids of the iron range and realized that the kindling, with one or two shaved pieces of wood, the matches—all of which he laid out in readiness each night before we retired—were being put to use. They were not going to enjoy *his* cup of coffee that morning! It was November and dark as a pocket in the forest. The fire in the ample wood furnace was at its lowest ebb.

It is strange that I have no further memory of Charley at Goose Bay. Whether this was the last incident of a last visit, I do not know.

Nor do I have any memory of a final farewell in Santa Barbara. There was an exhibition of some of Charley's paintings at one of the galleries. It was an unprecedentedly hot day in early April, and Nancy was pushing Charley about in view of an expected sale of a canvas—and possibly a commission. It was all exceedingly distasteful to me, and to us all—a regular jangle. I prefer to go back to those pleasanter winter evenings when the sea waves thundered on our shore while we played mah-

jongg with Nancy in the Russell cottage and Charley hovered
by with *"Kung, hung, chung, chung,"* a faked Chinese with
which he made mild fun of us and added as much flavor as did
the handsome pieces of the game which we moved about.

It was in Santa Barbara that my father was destined to realize
a last farewell with Charley. On the day of my father and mother's arrival for their next-to-the-last visit there, they received the
news that Charley was gone. It was for all of us as when the
1918 forest fire swept our beloved Point of land and its tallest
pine tree fell.

BY VERNE LINDERMAN[3]

I first became aware of an individual named Charles
M. Russell (Charley, as he was always referred to in our home)
when we were living in Helena. There was talk at the dinner
table of some project promoting the interests of Charley. Perhaps it was the commission to paint a canvas to hang above the
mantel in the reading room of the Montana Club, which my
father had engineered.

Evidently Charley had been in Helena previously, for he had

[3] Verne Linderman, the second daughter, attended Montana State University as an art major. She has been a newswoman since 1923, first in Kalispell,
Montana, and since 1930 with the Santa Barbara, California, *News-Press*. Now
semiretired, she is unmarried. In a letter to me dated April 5, 1963, Miss Linderman writes: "As a youngster my interests were never with the Old West but
with the far-off hills, and while I may have painted place cards with Charley
and enjoyed his stories, the artists I admired were in France. It is the same old
story. So I found that it wasn't too easy to do a sympathetic sketch."

painted the big mural in the House of Representatives at the capitol some years before. Although my father had obviously been largely instrumental in getting this commission also, Charley had not, to the best of my recollection, come to our home.

Now, however, I was of high-school age and more aware of what was transpiring in the world around me. I was half pleased that we knew an artist, but the rest of me rebelled when Charley, with his pretty wife, Nancy, came to our home on West Lawrence Street. This person, wearing rings on almost every finger, a cowboy hat and boots, and a red *voyageur* sash under the coat of his business suit, was an oddity, to say the least. There was something undeniably charming about him, but it was, to use a modern term, "offbeat."

The project, whatever it might have been, was a success. Since it helped seal a natural friendship, my father thereafter often visited Charley in Great Falls. There were hunting trips also, in which New York artists (of this I approved) participated. Illustrated letters came from Charley, badly misspelled and ungrammatical but replete with a wonderful wisdom and humor, I would later discover.

Once we went to Great Falls for a Christmas vacation, and I recall my father's eagerness that his daughters should be properly impressed with Charley's log studio at the rear of his and Nancy's house.

We heard also of medicine-smokes in the lodge in Great Falls of a chief named Big Rock. It was there, as well as in Helena and Washington, D.C., that the successful, though long drawn-out, campaign to find a reservation for the Rocky Boy tribe of

Chippewas was forwarded by my father, aided by such men as Theodore Gibson, Percy Raban and Charley Russell.

After my sister Wilda and I had been students at the State University of Montana for a year our family built a log house and moved to Flathead Lake, where my father could have quiet and leisure to get into book form the legends he had been collecting from Plains Indians. Some of these had already appeared in his *Indian Why Stories,* illustrated by Charles M. Russell.

Our first visitor at the lake was none other than Charley. We pitched a tipi for him on the north point of our bay, and on frosty mornings he would hobble over the uneven ground on his high-heeled boots, his breath white in the cold air, to return a pan in which mother had baked some biscuits for him, or to show us a flame-red moose-maple leaf. *Napi,* he said, had been painting.

One morning he caught us unpacking a trunk and removing some of our city clothing. He apparently felt sorry for three girls come to live in a wilderness, and, to make such amends as he could, he dressed himself in my white fox fur neckpiece and a big velvet hat. Charley had a heavy-featured face—not unlike an Indian face, although he was fair-haired and blue-eyed. The effect was ludicrous. His small eyes danced. I discovered for myself his famous humor.

In the evening, while mists half shrouded the moonlight in the October woods outside, Charley used the maple leaves for the skirts of ballet girls which he painted on a piece of my drawing paper as we made place cards together. (I had been an art student of sorts at the University.) When another and another place card had been finished, Charley exclaimed, "Yours look like kids, and mine look as old as the hills!" His characteristic nasal chuckle shook his body, he was so amused.

One March day in response to a letter we drove to Somers over muddy, rutted roads, to meet Charley, who had arrived via train wearing an overcoat and unbuckled galoshes like a flapper. He had the appearance of having been put on the train to be met at his destination like a child, and this was not far from the truth.

Often in the summer we drove to the Russell cabin on Lake McDonald, where fascinating elves, created by him from the cedar bark around the cabin, eyed us from porch railings and steps. Often, as he told us stories, he performed his by-then-famous trick of modeling a mountain goat or a coyote from a piece of clay in his pocket and bringing it out practically perfect.

In 1920 came a rupture in the friendship, which, however, endured unto the end, if in less whole-hearted state. My father was something of a hero-worshiper, and he had worshiped Charley. The latter was to illustrate my father's second book, *Indian Old-Man Stories.* Meantime, however, Nancy had engineered for him a commission to paint a canvas for the Canadian lodge of the then Prince of Wales, now the Duke of Windsor. It was to bring Charley something like $10,000. Nancy sent Charley down to Goose Bay, our home, to visit and to inform my father that he could not finish the illustrations until the commission was completed. Charley, tender-hearted, and perhaps lacking moral courage, could not bring himself to break the news and returned to Lake McDonald without a word.

131

Nancy then invited us to Lake McDonald to see that the news was voiced to my shocked father. It was then midsummer, and any delay in the illustrations would mean that the book could not appear in time for the Christmas trade; Scribner's therefore decided to hold it for a year.

This was disastrous for my father,[4] but a letter written by Charley at that time, and still in our possession, indicates that he either had no comprehension of what he had done, or willfully dodged its implications. He lightly suggested another publisher or another illustrator, although he promised to finish the illustrations eventually. Indicating that he had received a bitter letter from my father, he referred sympathetically to the loss we had suffered in a forest fire at Goose Bay, preferring to attribute the bitterness to hard luck, rather than to any contributing element of his.

Nevertheless, the winter of 1922–23 found us living side by side with Charley and Nancy, their adopted son Jack, and Charley's mother from St. Louis, on the edge of the sea in Santa Barbara, California.

There were many evenings together, and we were invited to many of the same homes, often with Santa Barbara's beloved Western artist, Edward Borein, whom Charley had known in New York, and his wife Lucile. On at least one occasion Charley did not deport himself as advantageously as Nancy would have

---

[4] About this time the finances of the Lindermans began to run low. Frank purchased the Hotel Kalispell, in the town of that name in Montana, ran it for two years, sold it, returned to the Goose Bay home, and once again settled down to write.

liked, and she ridiculed him in front of comparative strangers. I remember the dignity of Charley in situations such as these— his innate grace and charm a poignant contrast with the garb of a rougher milieu which he affected and loved.

At this period Charley often spoke vehemently against the current trend in art, the so-called "French School," the Impressionists. His denouncements were bitter. In our family evenings I warmly defended the new school, whose acquaintance I had made in a slight degree at the University of Montana and in the *International Studio* magazine. I recall my mother's displeasure that a daughter of hers would argue with someone older than herself and my father's support of Charley's viewpoint.

Meantime, Charley, backed by Nancy, was "arriving" through the medium of Hollywood. We heard of his triumphs but, having scant admiration for Hollywood, were likely to speak lightly of them in the bosom of our family.

In recent years, I have had the pleasure of meeting Ollie Carey, widow of the screen actor Harry Carey, of old silent and later talking movie days, and herself a screen and television figure. She has told me of the frequent visits of Charley and Nancy Russell to their 3,700-acre ranch at Saugus, which included a guest ranch. Douglas Fairbanks, Will Rogers, and practically every film notable of the day came there. The Russells, having much to gain, mingled with them and sold paintings and sculptures cast in bronze through these contacts. They were "in" and made fast friends. It was a happy, triumphant period for them.

A few years later, when my parents were again in Santa Barbara—this time alone—the news came to them of Charley's

133

death in Great Falls. In the years that followed he continued to live on in our home, where, among the pictures on the walls, were many of his illustrated letters, and where friends and strangers alike loved to hear Charley Russell stories, which my father loved to tell.

BY NORMA LINDERMAN WALLER[5]

I T seems, now that Charley Russell has become a part of the history of Montana, that little personal memories of him can no longer be claimed as one's own, that his public demands we share our memories with them.

First, I must tell you that to us girls Charley and Nancy Russell were always Mr. and Mrs. Russell. We grew up in that time when older people were never spoken to by first names. Mrs. Russell generally called him "Chas" and his name for her was "Mame." They came to visit us for the first time in the fall of 1911 after he received the commission to paint the capitol picture. I'm sure my father was as elated over Mr. Russell's good fortune as was Mrs. Russell. He had done all he could to help sell the Board of Examiners on the idea. This was Mr. Russell's first big order.

It must have been late October or early November when they came over to discuss final plans for the painting. I remember Mr. Russell's lamenting that his "shack" would never be the

---

[5] Norma Linderman spent one year at Montana State University before she became Mrs. Roy O. Waller. Now the mother of four children, she makes her home in Kalispell, Montana.

same when he raised the roof to accommodate the big painting. Evenings as we sat visiting in our living room I would see Mr. Russell pull one of his wee wax figures from his pocket. He would set a tiny pig with curly tail on the arm of his chair, giving it a punch here and there, and just as I was about to say "May I have it?" his deft fingers would flatten it out and drop it back into his pocket, to come out next as a cocky rooster, feathers and all. I never heard of anyone else who could do this.

I remember Daddy and Mr. Russell coming in for dinner one evening, both chuckling over their afternoon's work. Helena was preparing for a big Shrine parade, and all the men were busily painting costumes for camels and giraffes. Mr. Russell had contributed his bit by adding some spots to a giraffe costume. Daddy was telling us how amateurish all the other spots looked. Wouldn't some collector love to have that giraffe costume today!

Verne and I took our first snapshots of Mr. and Mrs. Russell that fall. Wilda was in Evanston, Illinois, with my father's brother. Mrs. Russell had an elaborate pink silk Chinese kimono with matching boudoir cap, a new feminine item that fall, and she allowed us to take her picture one early morning before we snapped some of Daddy and Mr. Russell.

When Mrs. Russell wanted Mr. Russell to do something he didn't want to do, she would drop on the floor at his knees, clasping her hands over his knees and looking pleadingly up into his face, and saying, "Please, Chas!" As young as I was, this seemed artificial. My parents didn't act that way.

During Christmas vacation that year Mother, Daddy, Verne, and I went over to Great Falls to visit the Russells. They only had room for Mother and Daddy so Verne and I slept at the Percy Raban home. One morning I had the privilege of watching Mr. Russell work on the Big Picture. As I entered the studio his back was toward me. He was squatted, Indian fashion, on an old kitchen chair and he grunted with each brush stroke.

Mrs. Russell wanted very much to be a part of the social whirl of Great Falls and had persuaded Mr. Russell to take dancing lessons. One part of our entertainment was a big holiday dance. Dressed in my first formal, and he in his dress suit, red silk sash, and cowboy boots, I danced with Mr. Russell. I couldn't say much for his waltzing, but how he loved the fox trot! Each step had the stealth of a fox. His eyes twinkled. One felt that it wasn't a dance to him but a ritual to the stealth of the fox and that he danced his partner into the land of the fox. That was one of the few times I felt close to Mr. Russell—I felt I understood him.

Our last night at dinner Mr. Russell presented Verne and me with models of colonial dames. They were dressed in the traditional style of the old South, but both had the features of Indian women.

They visited us again in January, 1913, when they came over to supervise the lighting of the capitol picture. After months of work my father had at last convinced the Montana Club Board of Directors that a Russell painting was a must for the Helena Club room, and on that January visit Mr. Russell received the Montana Club order, his second big commission. Mrs. Russell wrote Daddy, after the hanging of the Montana Club picture: "What do you think, we have sold three pictures to the Ford boys yesterday. Jerkline and two little blacktail deer pictures.

136

I think the Club and Maroney buy has livened things up a bit for us. Many thanks to you." Out of gratitude for Daddy's help Mr. Russell presented each of us girls with a cast plaster model. Mine was a coyote and Wilda and Verne each had a bear.

I didn't see Mr. Russell again until the fall of 1917, when we moved into the Goose Bay house and he gave us the name of "Swiss Family Robinson," even calling us the "Swissy Family." We were far from ready for visitors, Mr. Russell arriving with the packing boxes. Daddy pitched the Painted Lodge over on the Point for him, and there they cooked some of their meals over the lodge fire.

He was on hand to watch the movers set up our grand piano, and I can still hear his delightful chuckle when I impatiently told him to wait until I "unpried" this board before he tried to help. And then help he did, throwing the mirror base-board to Verne's mahogany dresser out under the porch with the discarded packing lumber. We didn't find it until spring came to Goose Bay.

The men had grown careless of their table manners with eating over the lodge fire, and one evening in the Goose Bay dining room both men reached for one of Mother's hot biscuits with their forks. We girls let Daddy know we did not approve. After dinner Mr. Russell registered in our new Guest Book with this remark: "Whales are harpooned, not biscuits." On another visit he painted a small scene of the Goose Bay woods after his registered name.

Mr. Russell visited us at Goose Bay fall and spring every year from 1917 to the fall of 1925. He always became just a part of the family, doing as he pleased, painting, reading, or falling asleep in the living room by the crackling fire, snoring like a herd of horses on stampede. One evening after dinner he said, "Well gals, I'll wash the dishes tonight." He really didn't mean it but Verne said "Fine," so he was caught. Always game, he splashed around in the dish-pan for nearly three hours, recounting tales of the old South and of a trip Mame and he had made to the Mardi Gras. He had that special art of being able to change his voice to fit the characters of his stories. I'm sure I never spent a more enjoyable time drying dishes.

In all that time we spent only one weekend at the Russell Cabin on Lake McDonald. I can't remember the year or month, but it was summertime. I remember most the spell his delightful wood gnomes cast over the approach to their cabin and the delight Mr. Russell expressed over the golden network formed by sunlight playing on the waters of Lake McDonald. I can recall little of the weekend at their cabin. It was always a disappointment to me.

We were together most during the winter that we were next door neighbors in Santa Barbara. We reached Santa Barbara in early October, and it was late November before Mr. and Mrs. Russell and Jack arrived. Our homes were just across the boulevard from the ocean. Santa Barbara was kind to people of the arts, and before the Russells came Mother and Daddy had been royally entertained. When the Russells joined us Daddy saw to it that they were invited to the many dinners and took delight in getting Mr. Russell to recount his adventures.

Together they put on a benefit show for the Indian Defense

Association of Santa Barbara. They pitched a tipi, borrowed from Ed. Borein, California's cowboy artist, on the stage. Mr. Russell and I were dressed in Indian costumes. I recall Mr. Russell insisted that I let him paint the part in my hair bright red, because that was the way Indian women dressed up for special occasions. I was only stage-dressing, sitting Indian fashion in the door of the lodge throughout the entire evening. Daddy carried the bulk of the program, telling stories about the cowboys, the Indians, and some in French-Canadian dialect. Mr. Russell told stories in the Indian sign language and Daddy acted as interpreter. They put on two performances before a packed house, making a very profitable donation to the Indian Defense Association.

One rather blustery evening after a day of rain we were invited over to the Russell house for dinner to welcome Mr. Russell's stepmother, who had just come to visit. Just before we were to sit down to eat, Master Jack vanished. Our homes were on a busy boulevard with cars rushing by in both directions. Fear was expressed for Jack's safety. Daddy took one side of the boulevard and Mr. Russell the other while the women waited anxiously at home. It seemed hours before the men returned, Jack between them. He had run off down the boulevard and on over to a big roundhouse. There they found him gleefully helping an engineer handle one of the old engines. Mrs. Russell banished him to bed at once minus his dinner, but gentler Mr. Russell couldn't help but show his amusement over Jack's adventure. It did Jack little good to be punished as he was, for no one checked to see if he stayed in bed. Far from it. He had sneaked back down the stairs and sat hidden on the bottom step listening to his father brag about his many pranks. Jack was a handsome little fellow, but contradictory ways of discipline spoiled him.

Mrs. Russell needed a secretary, and living next door, I was hired. I wouldn't say I was overpaid. I earned the fabulous amount of fifty cents an hour. One windy day I'd been taking and typing her correspondence, from early morning until late afternoon, finishing about four o'clock. When I finished they invited me to ride to the post office with them. Mr. Russell and I got out to mail the letters while Mrs. Russell drove off on another errand. The wind was whipping around the corners, and as we stood waiting a chance to cross State Street Mr. Russell exclaimed, "Look at that, look at that man's coat!" The wind had caught the front of his sport coat, blowing it back to show its bright red lining. "That's the way men should dress. We wear such drab clothes. Wish we could dress the way they used to in the old days—bright colored coats with lace collars, knee britches and shoes with big buckles on them. Wow! I'd really like that." And I secretly thought what a humorous picture he would make dressed in such a costume.

The next years seem to have slipped by with occasional meetings at Goose Bay or at John Lewis' Lake McDonald Hotel.

My last vivid picture of Mr. Russell was the fall of his last visit to Goose Bay. If I shut my eyes I can still picture Goose Bay drive carpeted in golden tamarack needles and see Mr. Russell advancing down the drive in his broad-brimmed hat, red sash swinging with his halting steps on those high-heeled cowboy boots, and hear his cheery greeting to Daddy, waiting at the house, "Ho! Ho! Hi-eeeeeee!"

INDEX

Adams, Ramon F.: xii
Ah-wah-cous (Horns that Fork, or Antelope) : *see* Russell, Charles M.
Alberta, Canada: 52
Alexander, John: 96n.
American: The Life Story of a Great Indian, Plenty-Coups, Chief of the Crows: xix

"Babe": *see* Waller, Norma Linderman (Mrs. Roy O.)
Barrows, John R.: 16–17
Bear Paw Pool: 23
Beyond Law: xxi
Big Rock (Indian chief): 129
Billings, C. K. G.: 83–85
Blackfoot Indians: ix f., xvi, xxiii, 52
Black George: 37–40
Blood Indians: ix, xxiii, 30n., 52&n.
Bonheur, Rosa: 84
Borein, Edward: 74–75, 106, 132, 139
Borein, Lucile: 132
Brandon, Mont.: xv
Britzman, Homer E.: xii
Browning, Mont.: xvii
Buffalo-Body, Mrs.: 43n.
Bull, C. L.: xviii
Bull's Head Lodge: 89n.; *see also* Lake McDonald
Butte, Mont.: x, xv